SCHOLASTIC
LITERACY
PLACE®

Acknowledgments and credits appear on pages 438–439, which constitutes an extension of this copyright page.

4 5 6 7 8 9 10   09   07 06 05 04 03 02 01 00

TABLE OF CONTENTS

SNAPSHOTS

THEME

Our actions tell about us.

UNIT 1

TABLE OF CONTENTS

Theme

There may be more than one way to solve a problem.

UNIT 2

TABLE OF CONTENTS

Lights! Camera! Action!

THEME

Creative teams produce great performances.

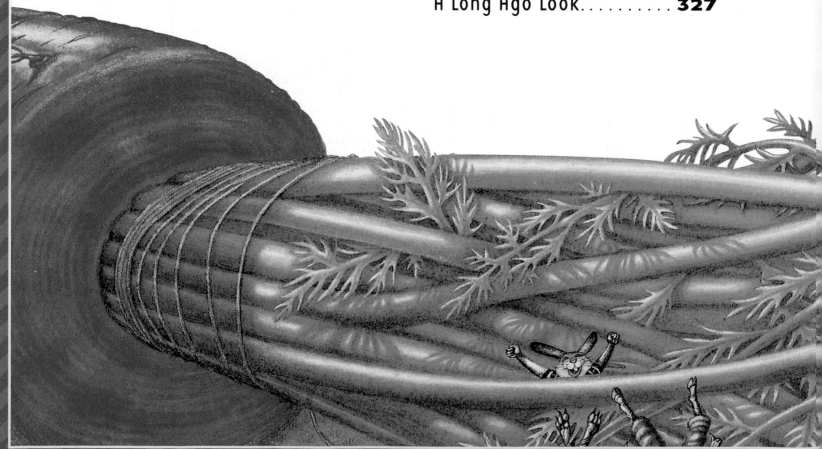

UNIT 3

SNAPSHOTS

SNAPSHOTS

THEME
Our actions tell about us.

www.scholastic.com

Visit the kids' area of **www.scholastic.com** for the latest news about your favorite Scholastic books. You'll find sneak previews of new books, interviews with authors and illustrators, and lots of other great stuff!

UNIT 1

Welcome to
LITERACY PLACE

Come to a Sports Arena

Our actions tell about us.

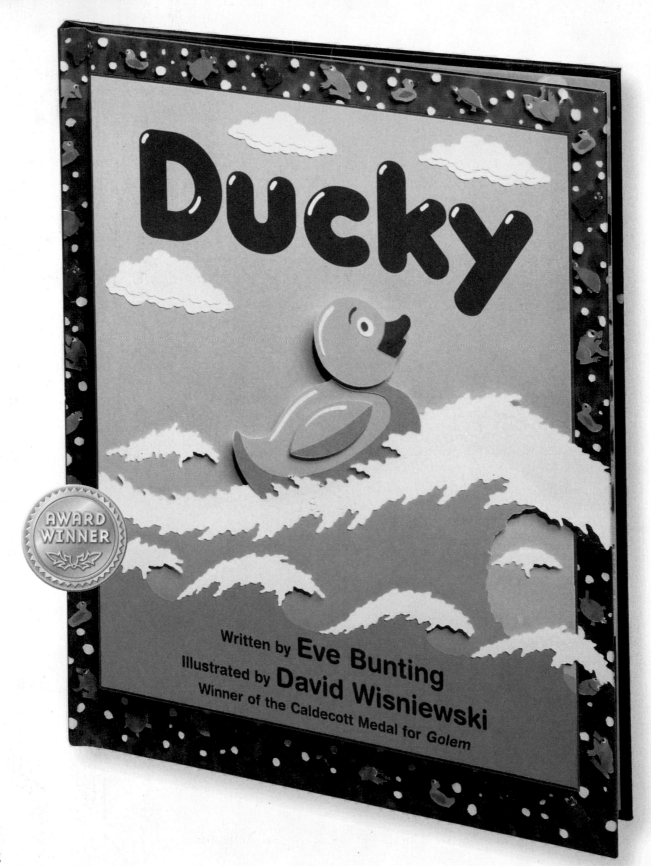

Written by **Eve Bunting**
Illustrated by **David Wisniewski**
Winner of the Caldecott Medal for *Golem*

I am a yellow plastic duck and I am in great danger.

Yesterday I was snuggled safe with hundreds of other bathtub toys. We were in a crate on a big ship.

A storm came.

Our crate was washed overboard.

DOWN

DOWN

DOWN it went.

We tumbled around inside,
yellow ducks, green frogs, blue
turtles, and red beavers.

BUMP

CRASH!

We hit bottom, the crate broke, and we bobbed
like colored bubbles to the surface.

14

15

The sun is rising now and the sea is pink.
My bathtub friends float all around me.
Our ship has disappeared.
The sea is big, big, big.
Oh, I am scared!

17

Fish with watery eyes come to stare.
A sea snake wiggles itself among us.
A great monster head rises close to me.
SHARK!
I go from scared to terrified.

The shark's mouth opens and it gulps in a frog, two beavers, three turtles, and me.

Things and bits of things are stuck in its giant teeth.

PFUH!

It shakes its head and spits us out. I expect we are not too tasty, though we are guaranteed non-toxic.

I wish we could swim and get away. But all we
can do is float.
It is a relief when the shark goes.

A wedge of pelicans flies above us.
Oh, how I wish I could fly! I'd fly to safety.
The frog next to me is turned upside down
by a wave, then right side up by another.

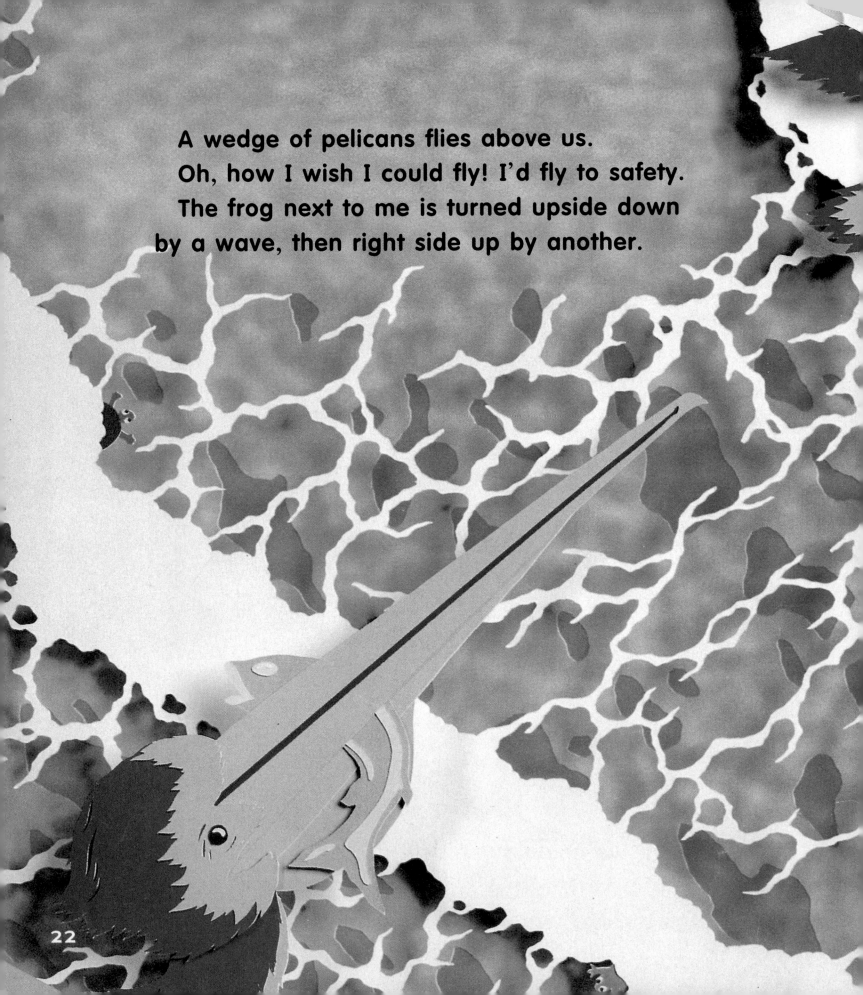

But we are drifting far from one another.
Great sea spaces separate us.
High on a sea swell I see us spread across
the ocean for miles and miles.

23

The next morning I have no yellow ducks, green frogs, blue turtles, or red beavers to keep me company. Like the ship, they have left, and I am alone.

25

I can't tell how long I float on the big, empty ocean.

There are days when sun sparks the water. When the ocean is blue with white ruffles.

There are days when I float through rain.

Days when wind blows me backward, tumbling me like a yellow ball. It is all the same to me. I only know the loneliness.

There are days when fog hides me even from myself. Then I am lonelier than ever.

There are nights of clouds and nights of
constellations.
There is a moon, and another and another.
The water must be colder now.
Ice nudges me.
Seals bark as I go by.
Will I float in this ocean forever and ever?

It is on a day of pale light that I feel the sea lift me, carry me, crash me down.

I'm somersaulting over small stones.

What is happening to me now?

Someone is shouting. "I've found one! I've found one! It's a duck!"

31

A boy's face is close to mine. We are nose to beak, beak to nose.

Another boy rubs my head. "Hi, Ducky!"

"That's what I'll call him, Ducky," my boy says.

His friend grins. "Good name. Very original."

"I need to report that I found him," my boy says. He gets on a bike. "Mrs. James is keeping a record for science."

For science? Me?

My gosh! Look at this!
It's great to see so many of my friends again.

Now we are in the room. My boy sets me on a table.

"I found him down on the beach, Mrs. James," he tells a woman.

"Thank you for reporting it," she says. She writes in a notebook. "I'll put it on my 'ducks found' list. People are finding a lot of these bathtub toys around town. The scientists are so interested."

"Ducky's coming home with me," my boy says.

We ride to his house and he puts me in his bathtub.

Oh, I am so happy!

I am a bathtub duck, fulfilling my destiny.

How wondrous it is to be able to float!

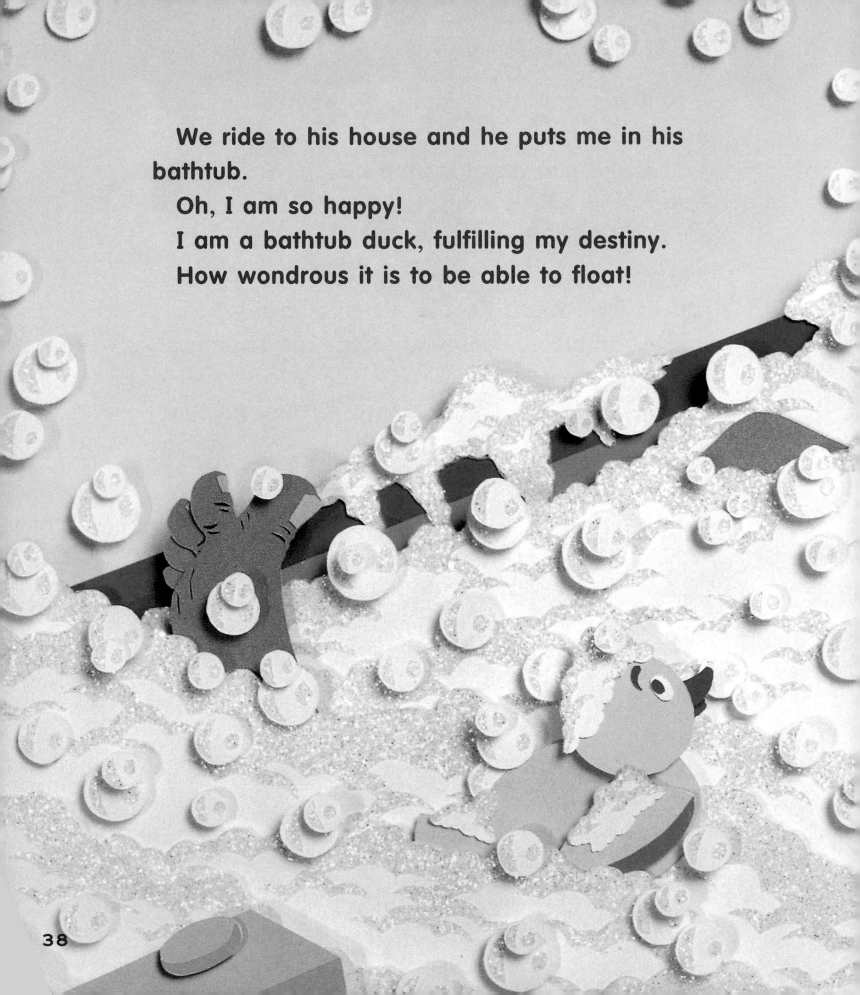

Think About Reading

Answer the questions in this story map. Do your work on another sheet of paper.

Character
1. Who is the main character?

⬇

Problem
2. How does Ducky feel when the ship disappears?

3. How does Ducky feel when a shark swims up?

4. How does Ducky feel floating all alone in the sea?

⬇

Ending
5. At last the boy puts Ducky in his bathtub. How does Ducky feel?

Write a Note

All alone on the sea, Ducky misses the other bathtub toys. Maybe he wishes he could send a note to those friends. What do you think the note would say? Write a note Ducky might send.

Literature Circle

Talk about when Ducky feels scared. Put yourself in Ducky's place. Would you have been as scared as Ducky? How else might you feel? What part of the journey would have been the most fun for you?

Author
Eve Bunting

What does it take to write a good book? Sometimes it takes a long, hot bath. That's what Eve Bunting thinks—and she's written more than 100 books. When Bunting has trouble working out a story, she likes to take a bath. While she's in the bathtub, she thinks about her story. Do you think she might have a yellow plastic duck in the tub, too?

More Books by Eve Bunting

- *Dandelions*
- *Twinnies*
- *Flower Garden*

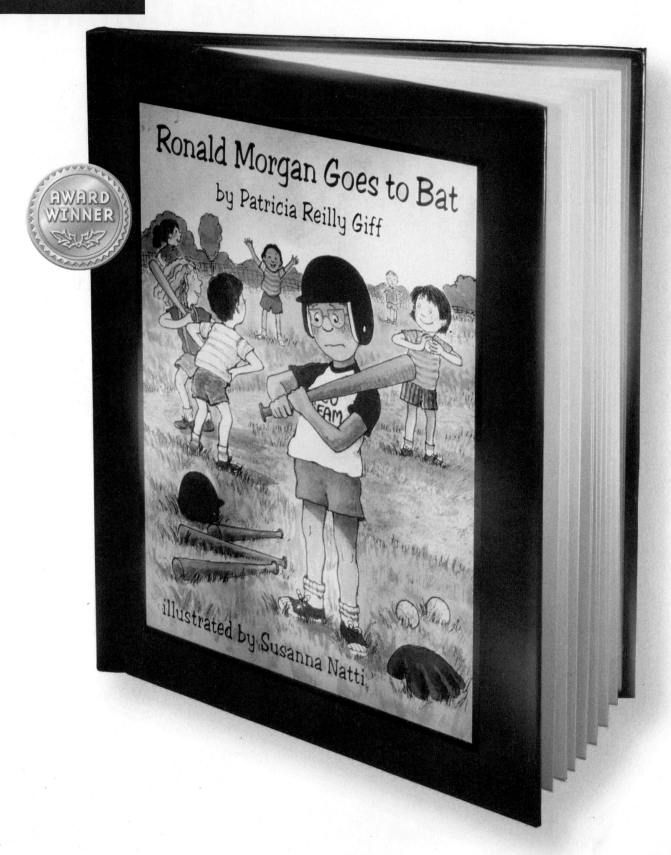

Ronald Morgan Goes to Bat

by Patricia Reilly Giff

illustrated by Susanna Natti

AWARD
WINNER

Baseball started today.

Mr. Spano said everyone could play.

"Even me?" I asked.

And Tom said,

"You're letting Ronald Morgan play?

He can't hit, he can't catch.

He can't do anything."

Mr. Spano looked at me.

"Everyone," he said.

"Yahoo!" I yelled.

I pulled on my red and white shirt,
the one that says GO TEAM GO,
and ran outside to the field.
"Two things," Mr. Spano told us.
"Try hard, and keep your eye on the ball."

Then it was time to practice.

Michael was up first.

He smacked the ball with the bat.

The ball flew across the field.

"Good," said Mr. Spano.

"Great, Slugger!" I yelled.

"We'll win every game."

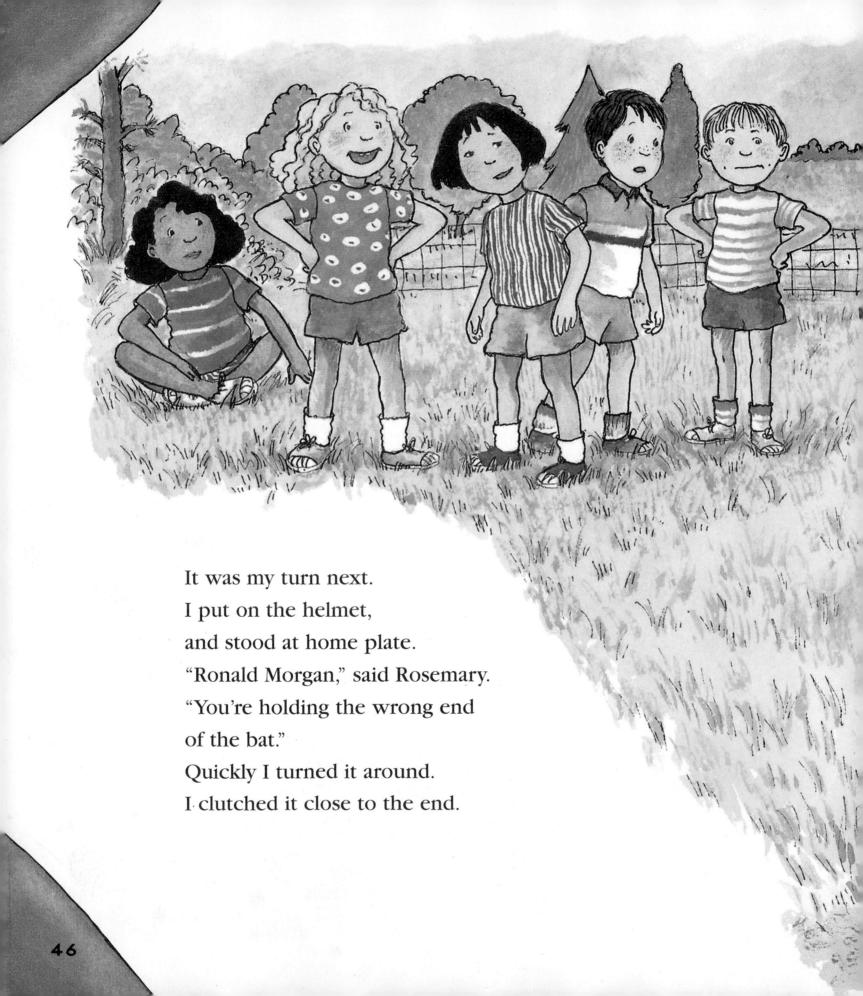

It was my turn next.
I put on the helmet,
and stood at home plate.
"Ronald Morgan," said Rosemary.
"You're holding the wrong end
of the bat."
Quickly I turned it around.
I clutched it close to the end.

Whoosh went the first ball.

Whoosh went the second one.

Wham went the third.

It hit me in the knee.

"Are you all right?" asked Michael.

But I heard Tom say,

"I knew it.

Ronald Morgan's the worst."

At snack time,

we told Miss Tyler about the team.

"I don't hit very well," I said.

And Rosemary said,

"The ball hits him instead."

Everybody laughed, even me.

I shook my head.

"I hope it doesn't happen again."

Miss Tyler gave me some raisins.

"You have to hit the ball

before it hits you," she said.

We played every day.

I tried hard, but the ball came fast.

I closed my eyes and swung.

"If only he could hit the ball once,"

Rosemary said.

And Billy shook his head.

I couldn't tell them I was afraid

of the ball.

"Go team go," I whispered.

One day, the team sat on the grass.
We watched the third grade play.
They were big, they were strong,
they were good.
Johnny hit a home run,
and Joy tagged a man out.

"We'll never hit like that," said Tom.

And Rosemary said,

"We'll never catch like that either."

But I said,

"Our team is the best."

Mr. Spano nodded.

"That's the spirit, Ronald."

Mr. Spano told us,
"Now we'll run the bases.
Rosemary, you can go first."
Rosemary went fast.
She raced for first base.
"Terrific, Speedy!" I yelled.

"Let me go next," I said.

"I can do that, too."

But the field was muddy.

My sneaker came off.

Jimmy said, "That kid's running
bases the wrong way."

And Tom yelled, "Ronald Morgan.
You're heading for third base."

The next day, we worked on catching.

I was out in left field.

While I waited, I found a stick,

and started to scratch out the mud.

I wrote G for go.

I wrote G for great.

Our team is the best, I thought.

Then I wrote H for hit.

H for home run.

If only I could do that.

Just then I heard yelling.

Someone had hit the ball.

"Catch it, Ronald!" Tom shouted.

I put down the stick.

I put up my mitt.

Too late.

The ball sailed into the trees.

Mr. Spano took us for ice cream.

"You deserve it for trying," he said.

"Our team is really good."

I had a chocolate cone.

Michael's a slugger, I thought.

And Rosemary can really run.

But I'm still afraid of the ball.

On the way home,

we saw some kids playing ball.

"Want to hit a few?" Michael asked.

I shook my head.

"Maybe I won't play ball anymore."

Michael said, "We need you.

You have spirit.

You help the team feel good."

"But how can we win?" I asked.

"I can't even hit the ball."

I saw my father and ran to catch up.

"See you, Michael," I said.

My father asked, "How's the champ?"

"I'm the worst," I said.

"I was the worst, too," said my father.

"But then…"

"What?"

My father laughed. "I stopped closing my eyes when I swung."

"Maybe that's what I do."

"How about a little practice?" he asked.

We went into the yard.

My father threw me some balls.

I missed the first one...

I missed the second.

And then...

I opened my eyes and swung.
Crack went the ball.
"Ouch!" went my father.
"You hit me in the knee."
"Home run!" yelled my mother.

"Sorry," I said.

"Hey, I did it!"

My father rubbed his knee.

"You certainly did," he said.

I ran to pick up the ball.

"See you later," I said.

My father smiled.

"Where are you going?"

I grabbed the bat.

"Some kids are playing ball.

I think I'll hit a few."

I looked back.

"And you know what else?

I guess I'll stay on the team.

I have spirit...

and sometimes I can hit the ball.

Mike was right.

I think they need me."

Babe Ruth

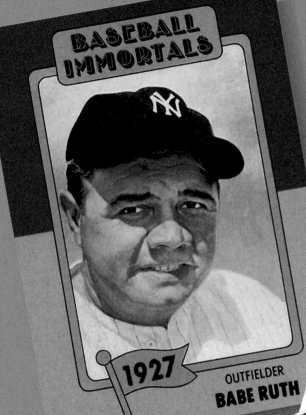

BASEBALL
IMMORTALS

1927

OUTFIELDER
BABE RUTH

Team:
New York Yankees

Born:
February 6, 1895

NEW YORK YANKEES OUTFIELDER
Born: 2/6/95 Died: 8/16/48
Height: 6'2" Weight: 215 Bats: L. Throws: L.

BABE RUTH

NO.
1

Considered by many to be the greatest player of all-time, Ruth revolutionized baseball by making the home run a major offensive weapon. Before Ruth's arrival, teams relied mostly on speed to score runs. In a 22-year career (1914-35), spent mostly with the Yankees, Ruth hit 714 home runs and a lifetime slugging average of .690. A .342 lifetime hitter, he ranks second on the all-time list in home runs and runs batted in and first in walks and slugging percentage. Ruth led the American League in home runs 12 times and his 60 homers in 1927 is the record for a 154-game season. Ruth also was a standout pitcher with the Red Sox before being shifted to the outfield.

Which Hall of Famer was known as "Double
X?"

Answer: Jimmy Foxx

Height: 6 feet, 2 inches
Weight: 215 pounds

Bats: Left
Throws: Left

Juan Gonzalez

Team: Texas Rangers

Bats: Right
Throws: Right

Height: 6 feet, 3 inches
Weight: 210 pounds

Born: October 16, 1969

COLLECTOR'S CHOICE

OF

Juan GONZALEZ • Rangers

630

JUAN GONZALEZ • OF

T

Height: 6'3" Weight: 210 lbs. Bats: Right Throws: Right Born: 10-16-69 Vega Baja, Puerto Rico

YR	TEAM	AVG	G	AB	R	H	2B		HR	RBI	BB	SO	SB
89	RANGERS	.150	24	60	6	9	3		1	7	6	17	0
90	RANGERS	.289	25	90	11	26	7		4	12	2	18	0
91	RANGERS	.264	142	545	78	144	34		27	102	42	118	4
92	RANGERS	.260	155	584	77	152			43	109	35	143	0
93	RANGERS	.310	140	536	105	166			46	118	37	99	4
5	TOTALS	.274	486	1815	277	497		5	121	348	122	395	8

Upper Deck and the card hologram combination are trademarks of The Upper Deck Company. © 1996 The Upper Deck Company. All Rights Reserved. Printed in the U.S.A.

Think About Reading

Answer the questions.

1. How does Ronald Morgan help his team?

2. Why does Ronald close his eyes when he is at bat?

3. How do you think Mr. Spano feels about having Ronald on the team? Why?

4. Ronald's father tells him, "I was the worst, too." How do you think that makes Ronald feel?

5. Why do you think Ronald and his friends would like baseball cards?

Write a Poster

Ronald Morgan wants lots of fans to come to his team's game. Make a poster about the game. Make up a time and place for the game.

- Write the time and place on your poster.

- Write a sentence that will make people want to see the game, too.

- Then draw a picture on your poster.

Literature Circle

How does Ronald Morgan change from the beginning of the story to the end? Have you ever felt the way Ronald Morgan did? In what way? Did your feelings change?

Author
Patricia Reilly Giff

When Patricia Reilly Giff was young, she wanted to be a writer. When she grew up, she became a teacher. She still thought about writing, though. She finally started to write stories that would make her students laugh. Now she thinks about real children every time she plans a story. She wants her books to help all children know that they are special.

More Books by Patricia Reilly Giff

- *Happy Birthday, Ronald Morgan*
- *The Beast in Ms. Rooney's Room*
- *The Postcard Pest*

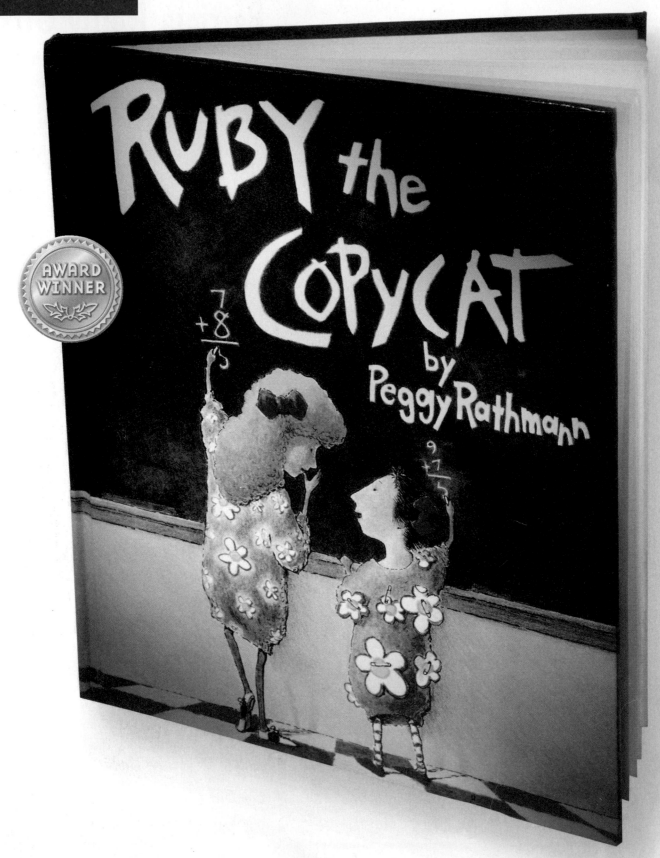

Monday was Ruby's first day in Miss Hart's class.

"Class, this is Ruby," announced Miss Hart.

"Ruby, you may use the empty desk behind Angela.

Angela is the girl with the pretty red bow in her hair."

Angela smiled at Ruby.

Ruby smiled at Angela's bow and tiptoed to her seat.

"I hope everyone had a pleasant weekend," said Miss Hart. "Does anyone have something to share?"

"I was the flower girl at my sister's wedding," said Angela.

"That's exciting," said Miss Hart.

Ruby raised her hand halfway. "I was the flower girl at my sister's wedding, too."

"What a coincidence!" said Miss Hart.

Angela turned and smiled at Ruby.

Ruby smiled at the top of Angela's head.

"Class, please take out your reading books," said Miss Hart.

At lunchtime, Ruby hopped all the way home on one foot.

When Ruby came back to school,
she was wearing a red bow in her hair.
She slid into her seat behind Angela.

"I like your bow," whispered Angela.

"I like yours, too," whispered Ruby.

"Class, please take out your math books,"
said Miss Hart.

On Tuesday morning,
Angela wore a sweater with
daisies on it.

At lunchtime, Ruby
hopped home sideways.

When Ruby came back to school after lunch,
she was wearing a sweater with daisies on it.
"I like your sweater," whispered Angela.
"I like yours, too," whispered Ruby.

On Wednesday, Angela wore a hand-painted
T-shirt with matching sneakers.

After lunch, Ruby hopped back to school wearing
a hand-painted T-shirt with matching sneakers.

"Why are you sitting like that?" whispered Angela.

"Wet paint," said Ruby.

On Thursday morning, during Sharing Time,
Angela modeled the flower girl dress she wore
at her sister's wedding.

Ruby modeled her flower girl dress, too,
right after lunch.

Angela didn't whisper anything.

By coincidence, on Friday morning, both girls
wore red-and-lavender-striped dresses.

At lunchtime, Angela raced home.

When Angela came back to school,
she was wearing black.

On Friday afternoon, Miss Hart asked everyone
to write a short poem.

"Who would like to read first?" asked Miss Hart.

Angela raised her hand. She stood by her desk and read:

I had a cat I could not see,
Because it stayed in back of me.
It was a very loyal pet—
It's sad we never really met.

"That was very good!" said Miss Hart. "Now, who's next?"
Miss Hart looked around the room. "Ruby?"

Ruby stood and recited slowly:

I had a nice pet,
Who I never met,
Because it always stayed behind me.
And I'm sure it was a cat, too.

Ruby smiled at the back of Angela's head.

Someone whispered. Ruby sat down.

"What a coincidence," murmured Miss Hart.

Angela scribbled something on a piece of paper.
She passed it to Ruby.

The note said:

YOU COPIED ME!

I'M TELLING MISS HART!

P.S. I HATE YOUR HAIR THAT WAY.

Ruby buried her chin in the collar of her blouse. A
big tear rolled down her nose and plopped onto the note.

When the bell rang, Miss Hart sent everyone home
except Ruby.

Miss Hart closed the door of the schoolroom
and sat on the edge of Ruby's desk.

"Ruby, dear," she said gently, "you don't need to
copy everything Angela does. You can be anything
you want to be, but be Ruby first. I like Ruby."

Miss Hart smiled at Ruby. Ruby smiled at
Miss Hart's beautiful, polished fingernails.
"Have a nice weekend," said Miss Hart.
"Have a nice weekend," said Ruby.

On Monday morning, Miss Hart said, "I hope everyone had a pleasant weekend. I did! I went to the opera." Miss Hart looked around the room. "Does anyone have something to share?"

Ruby waved her hand. Glued to every finger was a pink plastic fingernail.

"I went to the opera, too!" said Ruby.

"She did not!" whispered Angela.

Miss Hart folded her hands
and looked very serious.

"Ruby, dear," said Miss Hart
gently, "did you do anything else
this weekend?"

Ruby peeled off a fingernail.

"I hopped," said Ruby.

The class giggled.

Ruby's ears turned red.

"But I did! I hopped around the picnic table ten times!" Ruby looked around the room. "Watch!"

Ruby sprang from her desk.

She hopped forward.

She hopped backward.

She hopped sideways with both eyes shut.

The class cheered and clapped their hands
to the beat of Ruby's feet. Ruby was the best
hopper they had ever seen.

Miss Hart turned on the tape player and said,
"Follow the leader! Do the Ruby Hop!"

So Ruby led the class around the room,
while everyone copied *her*.

And at noon, Ruby and Angela hopped home for lunch.

from *Pass It On*

I Can

by Mari Evans
illustrated by Floyd Cooper

I can
be anything
I can
do anything
I can
think
anything
big
or tall
OR
high or low
W I D E
or narrow
fast or slow
because I
CAN
and
I
WANT
TO!

Think About Reading

Think about *Ruby the Copycat*. Do your work on another sheet of paper. Finish each sentence in the story map. Draw pictures to go with your sentences.

Beginning

First Ruby _____ .

Middle

Then Ruby _____ .

Ending

Finally Ruby _____ .

Write an Award

Everyone in class had fun doing the Ruby Hop! Suppose the other children give Ruby a special award. Make an award they might give her. Write these facts on your award:

- the name of the award
- the name of the winner
- a sentence about the winner

Literature Circle

How do you think the poem "I Can" would have made Ruby feel at the beginning of the story? How might her feelings have changed by the end of the story? How did Ruby learn to be herself? What else do you think Ruby might learn to be and do?

Author
Peggy Rathmann

Peggy Rathmann loves to draw! When she first worked on books for children, she illustrated stories that other people had written. Then she found out that she likes to tell stories, too. Now Peggy Rathmann draws pictures for stories that she writes.

Peggy Rathmann enjoys visiting schools. She reads stories to children and shows them how she draws pictures for her books.

More Books by Peggy Rathmann

- *Good Night, Gorilla*
- *Officer Buckle and Gloria*

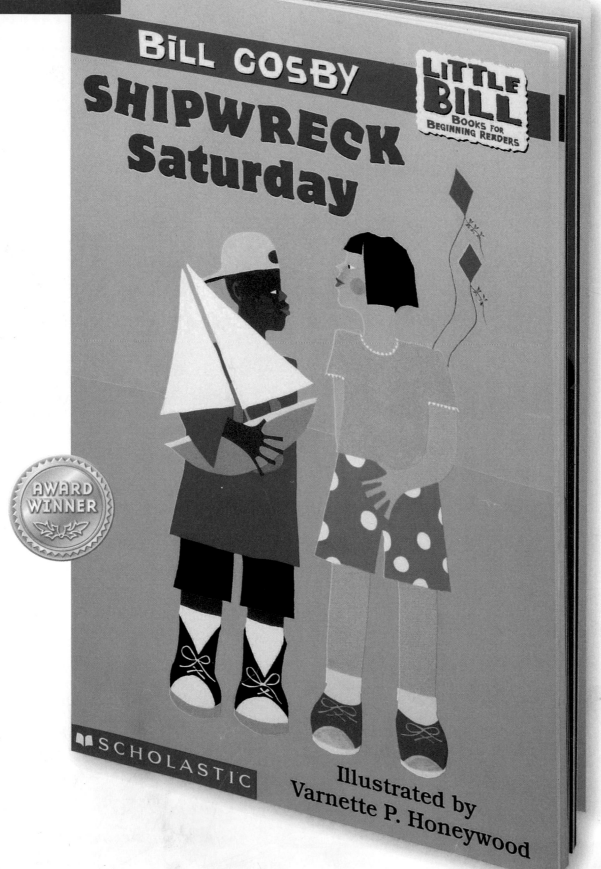

BILL COSBY

LITTLE
BILL
BOOKS FOR
BEGINNING READERS

SHIPWRECK
Saturday

AWARD
WINNER

SCHOLASTIC

Illustrated by
Varnette P. Honeywood

Chapter 1

Hi! I'm Little Bill. This is a story about a boat that I made all by myself. I named it *The Moby Dick*.

One Saturday morning, I woke up and saw that it was bright and sunny outside. Hurray! I could go with my brother to the park and sail my new boat.

I quickly got dressed and put on my baseball cap. First I put it on the right way. Then I put it on backward. I tried the brim on the side. Then I put it on forward again and pushed the brim down low. It looked very cool.

Running to the kitchen, I bumped into
my dad.

"Slow down," he said.

Mom pulled up the brim of my cap.
"You can't see a thing," she said.

I pushed it back down.

Mom pushed it up again.

Bobby and I ate breakfast while Mom packed a lunch for each of us — peanut butter and jelly on whole wheat bread, a banana, and a juice box.

"I'm going to try out the boat I made
last week," I said.

I finished breakfast first and pulled
Bobby away from the table.

"Be back by four o'clock," Mom said.

I grabbed my lunch, kissed Mom,
high-fived Dad, and ran out the door
behind Bobby.

Oops! I almost forgot my boat.

I ran back to my room and carefully took the boat off the shelf. I couldn't wait to test it out and show it off. I ran back outside to meet Bobby.

Chapter 2

Bobby's friends were waiting at the corner. We started to walk toward the park. "Hey, Little Bill. Did you make that boat?" Matt asked.

"Yes," I said proudly.

"You don't think it will sail, do you?" asked Brian.

I nodded. "Yes, I do."

"It will sail all right," said Matt, "right to the bottom of the lake."

That made me mad. I worked hard to make
my boat. And I was going to sail it!

I started to run as I got closer to the lake.

"I'll be at the courts," Bobby yelled. "I'll
check on you later."

I looked at the benches around the lake, and I saw a girl with a rainbow ribbon in her hair. It was my friend, Kiku, and she was with her grandmother.

"This is *origami*," Kiku's grandmother said, "the Japanese art of paper folding. You can make many things. Like a swan, a flower, and a fan."

Girl things, I thought.

"And boats," said Kiku's grandmother.

I showed them the boat that I had made.

"The sails are paper. The rest is wood," I said.

"Cool," said Kiku.

We walked to the lake. I carefully
placed *The Moby Dick* in the water.
The breeze caught its sails and it
floated away.

   Kiku warned me not to let it go out
too far. But I had a long roll of string.
I let the string out more and more until
The Moby Dick was in the middle
of the lake.

Suddenly, a rowboat came by. SWISH! The
ripples in the lake grew into waves. SPLASH!
A wave rolled over my boat. And SMASH! went
my boat into the other boat.

Kiku told me to rewind the string, but I was too shocked to move. Kiku took the string from my hand and pulled the boat in for me.

Her grandmother came over to us with two paper boats. But I didn't want to sail a paper boat. My boat was ruined. The mast was broken. The sails were soaked.

I didn't want Kiku to see me cry, so I ran home without my boat, without my lunch, and without my brother.

Chapter 3

At home, I threw myself on my bed and cried.

Dad came into my room. "What happened? Where's your brother? Where's your boat?"

I told Dad what happened. "You shouldn't have left the park without Bobby," he said.

I knew my dad was right. "I'm sorry," I said.

"Let's go to the park and see what we can do," said Dad.

I didn't want to go. Bobby and his friends would laugh at me. Kiku would laugh at me, too. "Do I have to go?"

My father nodded, "I think it would be best. Besides, I'll be with you."

At the park, I saw a crowd with Bobby
and his friends, Kiku and her grandmother.
I wanted to hide, so I pulled my baseball
cap down over my face. I didn't feel cool
anymore.

"Look," said Dad. He pulled the cap off
my face.

Everyone was looking up at a beautiful kite
that flew over the lake. The tail was made from
Kiku's ribbon, and the frame, Kiku told me, was
made from the sticks from my boat.

Kiku gave me the roll of string.

"That's a great kite," Bobby said.

"It's my boat," I said. "What's left of it."

"Cool, man," said Bobby.

131

Everyone laughed. And that was okay with me.

Go Fly a Kite!

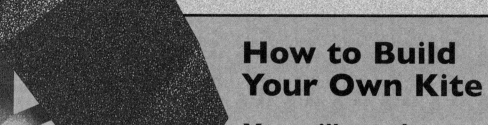

How to Build Your Own Kite

You will need:

- string
- scissors
- two pieces of paper
- a hole puncher
- a stapler

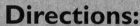

Directions:

1. Fold the first piece of paper. Cut off all four corners.

2. Fold the second piece of paper.

3. Cut out a piece from the middle of the folded paper.

4. Staple the second piece of paper to the first piece. Trim the edges with your scissors.

5. Punch holes. Tie a long string through the holes.

Wait for the wind. Then go fly your kite!

Think About Reading

1. Why does Little Bill want to go to the park?

2. Why is Little Bill so proud of his boat?

3. Why don't Kiku and Bobby and his friends laugh at Little Bill when he comes back to the park?

4. Why do you think Kiku gives the kite string to Little Bill?

5. What lesson do you think Little Bill learns?

Write a Question and Answer

What if Mom asked Little Bill about his day in the park? What do you think Little Bill would have told her? Write what he might have said.

Mom asked, "What happened today?"

Little Bill answered, "_____."

Literature Circle

What happens in each chapter of *Shipwreck Saturday*? If you could add a chapter to *Shipwreck Saturday*, where would you put it? What would happen?

Author
Bill Cosby

Do TV stars really write books for children? Most of them don't, but Bill Cosby does. Many people call Cosby "the funniest man in our country." He is a comedian, a TV and movie star, and a TV producer. He has written several very funny books for grown-ups, too. Now Cosby is also writing books about Little Bill for kids.

More Books by
Bill Cosby
- *The Best Way to Play*
- *The Meanest Thing to Say*
- *The Treasure Hunt*

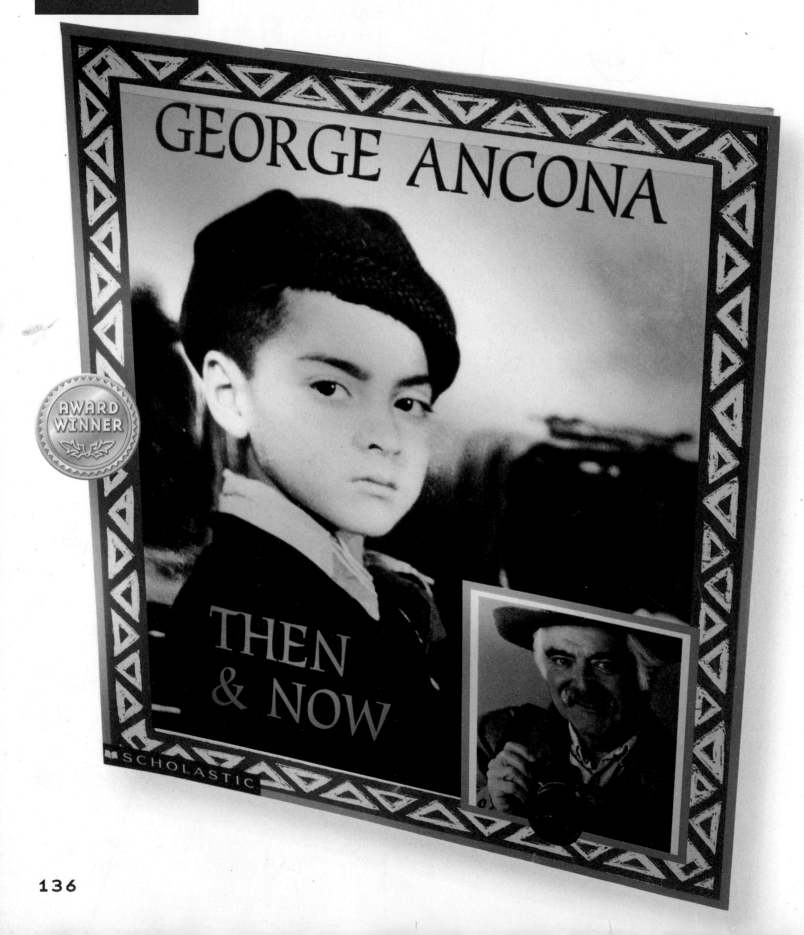

GEORGE ANCONA

THEN & NOW

AWARD WINNER

SCHOLASTIC

Mom, Neri, Dad, and me

Me,
4 months old

My parents came to the United States from Mexico
before I was born. They spoke only Spanish at home.
They named me Jorge (**hor** hay), but they called me
Jorgito (hor **hee** to). My friends in school called
me Georgie.

Now I am known as George Ancona.

137

Mommy and me at Coney Island

My family lived in Coney Island near the beach and the amusement park. When I was little I rode the painted ponies on the merry-go-round. Later, I painted pictures of them. My family would look at my pictures and say, "Jorgito is going to be an artist when he grows up!"

Painted ponies, age 20

Wild mustang, New Mexico

Now I am a photographer.
I look at the world through my camera.

Up to our necks in sand!

A sailor on wheels

Coney Island summer

140

Growing up in Coney Island was exciting.
There was always so much to do and see there.
I loved the sight of the ocean by day and the
bright lights on the rides at night.

I still love to look at the world all around me.

Watching and waiting to take a picture

Dressed for make-believe

As a child, I was always using my imagination. I had an older cousin who gave me the clothes that he outgrew. My favorite things were an aviator helmet and a pair of knee-high boots. Wearing these, I flew make-believe airplanes around my living room.

Now I use my imagination when I take my photographs and write my books.

Click!

Tio Mario, Neri, and me

My uncle, Tio Mario, worked in a sign shop, which I often visited. I loved watching him mix colors in big buckets of paint. He would take a can of yellow, pour in some blue, and mix it. I was amazed when the paint turned green right before my eyes.

Now I'm still amazed when I look through the camera and see something wonderful.

Fancy dancer at Crow Fair, Montana

Dad, me (circled), and the neighbors

My father's hobby was photography.
I explored the city with him on weekends.
We walked along the docks and watched big ships
bringing cargo into the port. While my father
took pictures, I daydreamed about faraway places.
I never thought I would become a photographer, too.

Now I travel all over the world taking photographs
of exciting places.

In a rain forest in Brazil

My grandma,
Chichi Neri

Mérida, diciembre 1º de 1931.

Niño Jorge Efraín Ancona Díaz.
New York.

Mi idolatrado hijito:
El día 4 del presente al cumplir
tus dos años de edad hubiese dado gustosa algunos de

Letters link my grandma
and me

My first trip to Mexico

When I went to Mexico as a young man,
I met my grandmother for the first time.
She had been writing to me from the day
I was born. Her handwriting was as beautiful
as the things she wrote. Through her letters
she shared her life story with me.

Now I share my life stories with my own children,
grandchildren . . .

My son Pablo and me

Mexico

Honduras

U.S.A.

. . . and children
all over the world.

U.S.A.

Brazil

Honduras

151

Bruce Thorson

Photographer

**Taking pictures is fun.
SNAP that SHOT!**

Have you ever taken a picture of something special to you? Photographers take all kinds of pictures. Good photographers take pictures that show something about themselves.

Bruce Thorson is a photographer. He takes pictures for an Oregon newspaper.

Questions

for Bruce Thorson

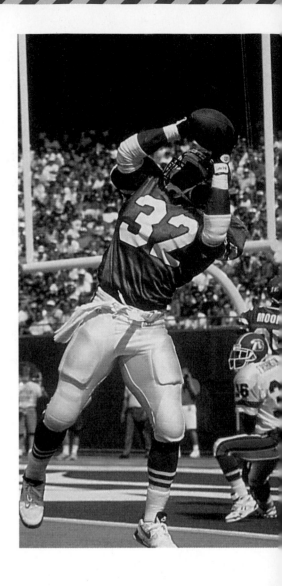

Here's how photographer Bruce Thorson shows who he is through his photography.

Q **How long have you been taking photographs?**

A I've had a camera since I was nine years old. I've always loved taking pictures.

Q **What is your job like?**

A There's a lot of variety. I drive to a lot of different places. I take pictures of people doing interesting things.

Q **What is your favorite thing to photograph?**

A Sports. I love football, basketball, and track because there is a lot of action.

Q **What do you think your photography tells people about you?**

A People say I have an eye for showing what an event was all about. And I guess a lot of my shots show that I love sports!

Bruce Thorson's Tips for Making Pictures

1 Carry a camera or paper and markers wherever you go.

2 Watch an activity for the moment that shows it best.

3 Practice. Make pictures of your friends doing things they like.

Think About Reading

1. What job does George Ancona's family think he will have when he grows up? Why do they think that?

2. Look at the pictures of George Ancona as a little boy. Who do you think took them? How do you know?

3. How does George Ancona share his life stories with children all over the world?

4. Look again at the photographs of the children on pages 150 and 151. How do you think they felt about having their pictures taken?

5. How is George Ancona's work like Bruce Thorson's work? How is it different?

Write a Caption

George Ancona wrote about himself as a boy and as a man. Think about your life right now. What is special about you? Draw a picture to answer that question. Then write a caption to go with your picture.

Literature Circle

How do George Ancona's photographs help him tell the story of his life? What special events would you show pictures of to tell about your life?

Author
George Ancona

When George Ancona was a little boy, he spoke Spanish with his family. Now, when he travels, he meets people who speak many different languages. He writes most of his books in English. In some of his books, Ancona uses both English and Spanish, side by side.

More Books by George Ancona

- *The Piñata Maker/El Piñatero*
- *Helping Out*
- *My Camera*

SUPER SOLVERS

THEME
There may be more
than one way to
solve a problem.

UNIT 2

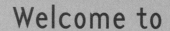

Welcome to

LITERACY PLACE

Tour a Toy Company

There may be more than one way to solve a problem.

from

ONCE IN A WOOD
TEN TALES FROM AESOP

Adapted and illustrated by

Eve Rice

BELLING THE CAT

A hungry cat had come to stay
and all the mice lived in fear.
The mice decided
they would call a meeting.

When they were
all together,
the biggest mouse
stood up and said,
"There is a hungry cat about.
As long as he walks these woods,
not one of us is safe.
So I ask you all to think.
What are we to do?"
Then one mouse gave a plan.
And one mouse gave another.
And still a third had his say
and on and on until
a very young mouse spoke.

"Friends," he said.
"I think that we can
solve this problem easily:

Hang a bell on the cat.
Then we will know when he is near
and we can stay out of his way."

"A good idea!" someone called.
And all the other mice agreed.
"We'll be safe at last!" they said
and danced around until
a very old mouse spoke.

"Friends," he said.
"One moment, please.
Things are easier said than done—
the old and wise will tell you that.
So now, will someone tell me this:
Who is going to bell the cat?"

Kids ™
Helping Kids

Friends

Photos by Julie Bidwell
Illustration by Maja Anderson

Dear Kids,
  I have a big problem.
I don't have any friends
at my new school. I
don't know what to say
to other kids, so most
of them think I'm stuck
up. When I try to join
them at recess, they
just walk away. No one
likes me, and I can't
stand it. What should
I do?

Jessica B.
Texas

We asked our Kids Helping Kids panel about Jessica's letter. Here are the panel's ideas.

JESSE
Maybe the kids are a little shy around someone new. Maybe there's another new person at school you could get to know first.

ADAM
Keep asking to play. They will let you.

ANDREA
Ask yourself why you are so scared. You know that you're new there, and you can't expect to get to know kids right away.

MICHAEL
Find something to do by yourself, like jump rope. Someone may want to join you after all.

KA'LISHA
If they walk away from you, just let it go. Making friends takes time.

YEISSMAN
Joining a club will help you get to know other kids, and they'll get to know you, too.

169

When the Sitter JUST SITS

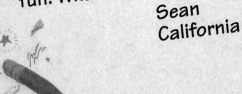

Dear Kids,
Please help. My baby sitter never spends any time with me. She picks me up and brings me home. Then she sends me upstairs to do my homework. Then she plops down on the couch and watches TV or talks on the phone. When my homework is all done, she never wants to do anything fun. What can I do?

Sean
California

JESSE

You should talk to her and ask why she doesn't want to do anything fun. Maybe you could change the schedule to make time for things she'll enjoy doing with you. She may want to help with your homework if you ask her. Maybe you could ask the sitter to come up with ideas to help pass the time.

MICHAEL

Your mother is paying her to keep you company. If she doesn't, then tell your mother what's going on. I don't think she'll want to lose her job. Make the TV off-limits for everyone.

ANDREA

Maybe there are games she'd like to play if you ask her. Maybe you can go over to a friend's house to play or ride a bike. Or you can ask your parents for another sitter because this one just isn't interested in you.

ADAM

Ask your parents for permission to watch TV after your homework is done. Tell your parents that you want to watch your TV shows, not just the ones the sitter likes.

YEISSMAN

Talk to the sitter and tell her you want to do something fun. If that doesn't work, just keep trying. Tell her you're bored and you need something to do. Maybe your parents have some ideas to make the time more fun for both of you.

KA'LISHA

Find something to do on your own. You have rights, too. See if you can play with your friends when the sitter is there. Maybe you and the sitter can cook together.

THINK ABOUT READING

1. Who is causing a problem for the mice?

2. Why do the mice have a meeting?

3. Why do so many mice like the idea of hanging a bell on the cat?

4. What do you think would have happened if the very old mouse had not spoken up?

5. How do you think the panel from "Kids Helping Kids" would help the mice in "Belling the Cat"?

WRITE A PARAGRAPH

Imagine you are the cat. You are listening when the mice have their meeting. What do you think about their plan? Write a paragraph about it.

LITERATURE CIRCLE

In the fable "Belling the Cat," a young mouse comes up with a solution to the problem. Does the solution work? Why? What lesson does the fable teach?

AUTHOR
EVE RICE

The story of "Belling the Cat" is very old. We know that it was told by Aesop in Greece about 2,500 years ago. He may have made the story up, or he may have heard it before. Eve Rice liked the story so much that she wanted to tell it again, with her own pictures.

More Fables by Aesop

- "The Tortoise and the Hare"
- "The Lion and the Mouse"

REALISTIC FICTION

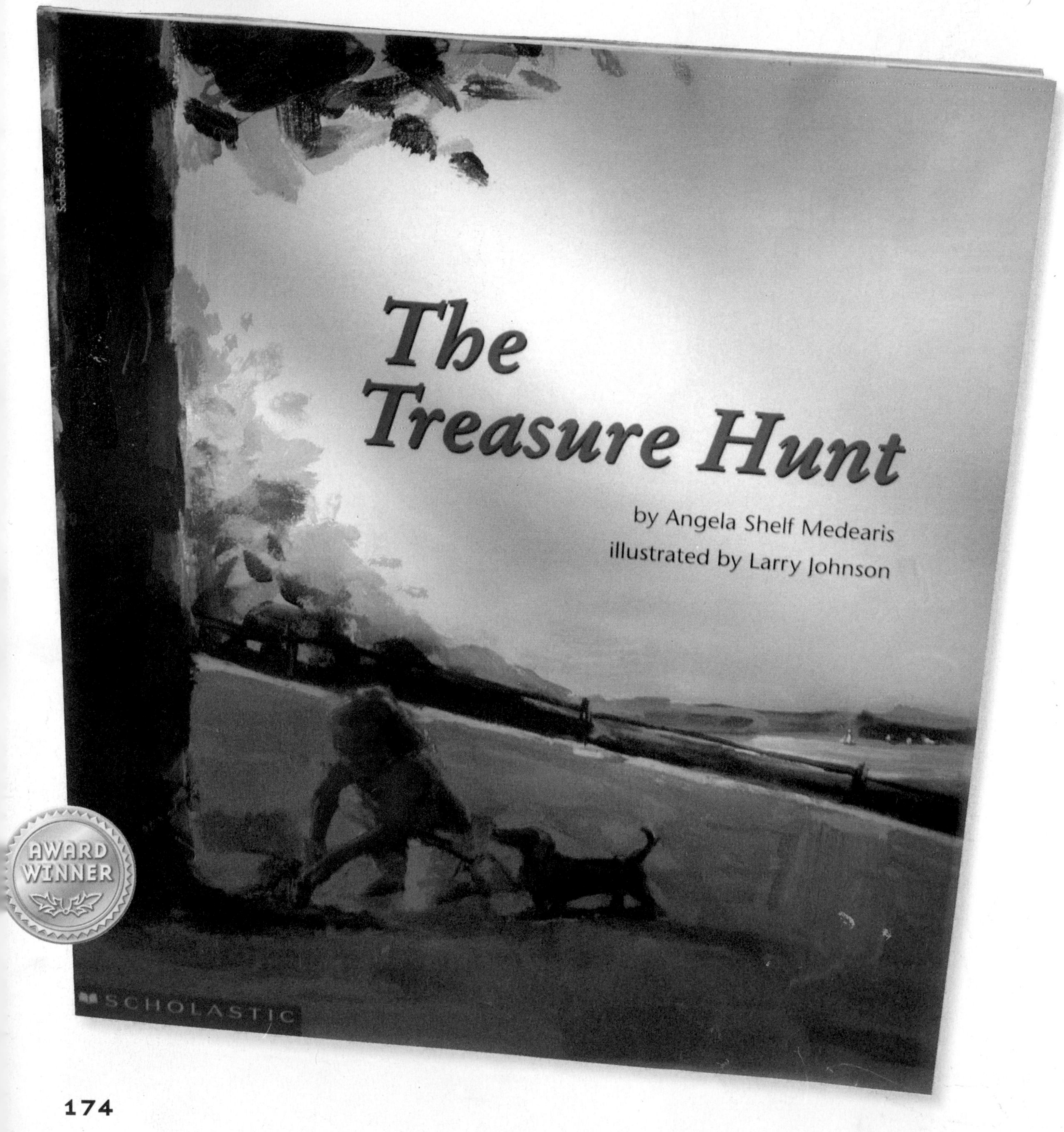
The Treasure Hunt
by Angela Shelf Medearis
illustrated by Larry Johnson
AWARD WINNER
SCHOLASTIC

Marcy pushed open the door to her big sister's room. She could see Annie sitting at her desk, bent over a notebook. Annie's pen was moving quickly across the page.

Marcy sat on her sister's bed and watched Annie
write. Marcy began to hum a little song.

Annie put down her pen. She looked at Marcy.
Marcy smiled and stopped humming.

"Will you play a game with me?" Marcy asked
sweetly. "You can go first."

"Just one game," Annie warned. "Then you
are going to leave, and I am going to finish writing
my story."

Marcy pulled her favorite game down from the shelf. Together, the two girls opened the game board and set up the pieces. They took turns moving their markers around the board. The game did not last very long. Annie won.

"You cheated," Marcy said to her sister.

"I did not!" Annie groaned. "You say that every time we play! Now go on. I want to finish writing my story."

Annie went back to her desk. She opened the notebook and started to write.

Marcy peeked over her sister's shoulder. "What's your story about?" she asked.

"I'm writing about a secret treasure," Annie explained. "The girl in the story solves a mystery and finds lots of gold buried under a tree."

"That sounds like a good story," said Marcy. "Can I read it?"

"Not yet!" Annie shook her head. "You can read it when it's done."

"But I want to read it right now," Marcy said as she reached for the notebook.

"Well, you can't," Annie told her, pulling the notebook back. "Leave me alone, Marcy!"

"Okay! Okay!" Marcy shouted, "Keep your old story! I'm going to find some real buried treasure!"

Marcy ran outside and into the backyard. She
climbed onto a swing and kicked her feet hard. The
swing carried her high in the air. She could see over
the fence and down the hill. In the distance Marcy
could see the lake in the park, where some people
were fishing.

Biscuit, Marcy's dog, came out into the yard. Marcy stopped swinging and patted Biscuit on the head. The dog wagged his tail. Then he curled up to take a nap under a tree.

Suddenly, Marcy had an idea. She got a shovel and a jar and started to dig right next to where Biscuit was trying to sleep.

"Wake up, Biscuit!" Marcy said. "I'll bet there's a treasure buried underneath this tree. Let's see if we can find it!"

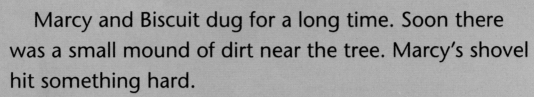

Marcy and Biscuit dug for a long time. Soon there was a small mound of dirt near the tree. Marcy's shovel hit something hard.

"A treasure!" Marcy yelled, and she dug deeper and deeper. At last she could see what it was.

"Oh," Marcy said sadly. "It's only a bone."

Biscuit was not disappointed. He took the bone, lay down, and chewed happily.

Marcy started digging again. Her shovel scooped up damp, dark dirt. Worms wiggled out of the dirt. The worms were getting in Marcy's way.

Marcy looked over the fence and down at the lake and sighed. "I found an old bone for you," she told Biscuit. "And I found lots of wiggly worms. What kind of a treasure is that?"

Then Marcy had a new idea. She got more jars
from the garage and started to fill them with worms.
She found a big box and carefully put the jars full of
worms into the box.

Annie called from the window, "I'm finished with
my story, Marcy. You can read it now."

"Sorry, Annie! Now I'm busy." Marcy answered.
"I'll read it later."

Marcy found some paper and a pen and made a
big sign. She carried the box and sign around to the
front porch.

Soon some neighbors came by and read her sign.

"This is just what I need," said Mr. Stevenson from next door. "I'll take two jars." He took out two dollar bills and gave them to Marcy.

"The whole family is going fishing this afternoon," said Mrs. Martínez from down the street. "I'll take five jars." She handed Marcy a crisp five-dollar bill.

Marcy sold every jar in the box.

After she took down her sign and cleaned up, Marcy went into the kitchen to count her money.

When Annie came into the kitchen for a snack, she saw Marcy sitting at the table.

"Where did you get all that money?" asked Annie.

"Oh," said Marcy, "I found some treasure buried in the backyard."

"But there is no treasure in the backyard," Annie said. "That only happens in stories."

"That's not true," Marcy told her sister. "You can find a treasure if you know where to dig!"

My Story: Angela

Angela Shelf Medearis is an author who remembers what it's like to be a kid. She says:

Many of my best story ideas come from things that happened to me when I was little.

ANNIE'S GIFTS
by Angela Shelf Medearis

Shelf Medearis

Ms. Medearis's father used to tell her stories about long ago when their people were kings and queens in Africa. In Medearis's book called *Our People*, a little girl has a father who tells her wonderful stories about real African and African-American heroes.

When Ms. Medearis was little, her mother called her Annie. In two of her books, a character named Annie does things based on what really happened to the author. In *Annie's Gifts*, Annie tries and tries to find an instrument she can play. *The Treasure Hunt* tells what happens when Annie's little sister Marcy wants to play and Annie does not.

Like the Annie in her stories, the author started writing when she was very young. "Any child who writes is a writer," says Ms. Medearis. "Writing is something you can do at any age—I love that about writing! Anybody can do it, and every one of us has something interesting to say!"

Think About Reading

1. At the beginning of the story, what does Marcy want Annie to do?

2. What two things does Marcy dig up in the backyard?

3. How do you think Marcy feels when neighbors start buying the worms?

4. Where do you think Marcy got the idea for selling worms?

5. Why do you think the worms were a treasure to Marcy?

Write a Radio Ad

Marcy likes selling worms. To tell more people about her worms, Marcy plans to read an ad on the radio. Write what Marcy might say in her radio ad that would make people want to buy her worms.

WORMS FOR SALE Cheap!

Literature Circle

How is the character Annie in *The Treasure Hunt* like Angela Shelf Medearis? Why do you think Medearis used a character like herself in this story?

Illustrator
Larry Johnson

Larry Johnson is a talented artist, and he uses his talent in many ways. He draws sports cartoons for magazines and newspapers. He designs art for T-shirts. He also creates illustrations for children's books.

More Books Illustrated by
Larry Johnson

- *When Joe Louis Won the Title*
- *Train*
- *Football Jokes and Riddles*

Pigsty
by MARK TEAGUE

onday afternoon Wendell Fultz's
mother told him to clean his room.
"It's turning into a pigsty," she said.

Wendell went upstairs. Much to his surprise, a large pig was sitting on his bed.

"Pardon me," said Wendell. He shoved some toys into his closet. But the pig didn't seem to mind the mess, and Wendell found that he didn't mind the pig, either.

He decided to take a break.

When Wendell's mother came to look at his room, the pig was hiding, but the mess was still there. She threw up her hands.

"Okay, Wendell," she said. "If you want to live in a pigsty, that's up to you."

Wendell could hardly believe his luck. "Now I can live however I want."

He didn't even worry when he came home on Tuesday and found a second pig in his room. The mess had grown a bit worse, but he was able to jam most of it under his bed.

"Pigs are all right," he said, "as long as it's only one or two."

In fact, they had a wonderful time. They played Monopoly until late each night . . .

. . . and left the pieces lying all over the floor.

They had paper airplane wars and pillow fights.
The bed became a trampoline.

Then two more pigs showed up.
The mess just grew and grew.

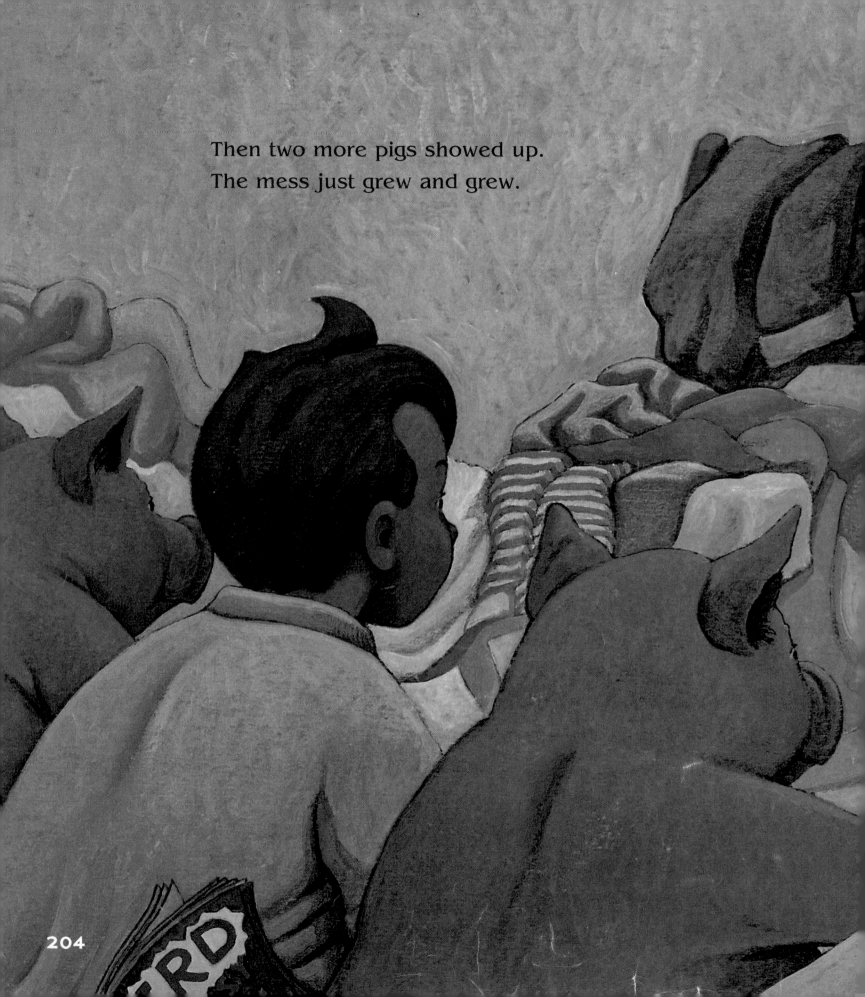

That night when Wendell went to bed, the pigs
were lying everywhere. They rolled up in his
blankets and hogged his pillows, too.

Wendell told himself he didn't mind, but
then he found hoofprints on his comic books.

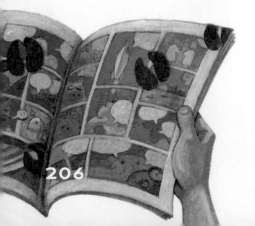

And Friday when he got home from school, he saw
that someone had been sitting on his basketball.
And his baseball cards were chewed.

"That does it!" said Wendell. "I've had enough!"
He ran downstairs to tell his mother.

"Sorry," she said, "but your room is your
responsibility." She handed him a broom.

Wendell started to complain. The mess was too huge. But suddenly he remembered a saying he'd heard, that "many hooves make light work."

He marched upstairs and organized a cleaning crew.

They swept and scoured, polished and scrubbed.

Later that afternoon, Wendell inspected his room
and pronounced it "clean."

In fact, it was a bit too clean, from a pig's point
of view. So while Wendell inspected, the pigs
prepared to go home. One of them made a
phone call, and a farm truck came to pick
them up. They hugged and grunted and oinked
"good-bye."

From that day on, Wendell kept his room clean . . .

. . . except for those nights
when his friends came by
to play Monopoly.

Think About Reading

Think about *Pigsty*. Do your work on another sheet of paper. Finish each sentence in the story map. Draw pictures to go with your sentences.

In the beginning of the story, _____ .

In the middle of the story, _____ .

At the end of the story, _____ .

Write a Postcard

After the pigs went back to their farm, they missed Wendell. Maybe they sent him a postcard from the farm. Make a card for the pigs to send to Wendell. Draw a picture on one side. On the other side, write what the pigs might write to their friend.

Literature Circle

What other stories have you read that remind you of *Pigsty*? How are these stories like *Pigsty*? How are they different?

Author / Illustrator
Mark Teague

When Mark Teague was in second grade, he wrote his own books. He loved drawing pictures for his books, too. When he was older and wanted a job, he didn't know what to do. He remembered the fun he had making books when he was young. Now he has fun writing and illustrating books again, and that's his job!

More Books by
Mark Teague

- *Lost and Found*
- *Baby Tame*
- *How I Spent My Summer Vacation*

MARTÍ
AND THE
MANGO

DANIEL MORETON

Martí lived on a small island, in a tiny house, at the base of a very tall tree.

Martí was a simple mouse, whose life consisted of simple pleasures: spending time with his best friend Gomez, afternoons in the sun, and a good imported Swiss cheese every now and again.

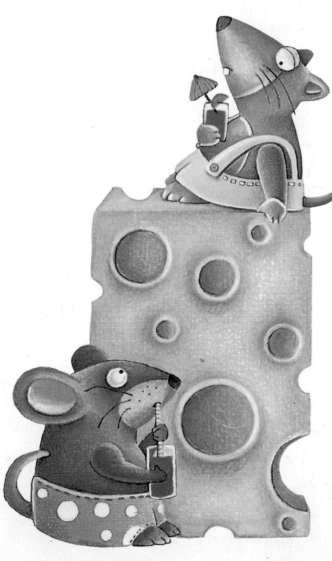

One day, however, Martí was faced with a rather extraordinary task.

He awoke as usual, and, as usual, he did his morning exercises. But when he went outside, he found a note from his friend Gomez tacked to the front of his door.

Dinner Tonight at my house. Bring a mango. —Gomez

"A mango?" thought Martí. "Who ever heard of such a thing? What does a mango look like?" he wondered. "And where on earth can I get one?"

Martí was a very curious mouse.

Quickly, Martí put on his lucky shirt and headed out in search of this mysterious mango. First he decided to stop next door at the lily pond, where his neighbor Frog was on his way out.

"Excuse me," said Martí.
"What's a mango?"

"A mango is a fruit!" Frog said, and—KERPLUNK—disappeared into the pond.

"Now we're getting somewhere," thought Martí. He took out his notebook and made a note that a mango is a fruit, and went on.

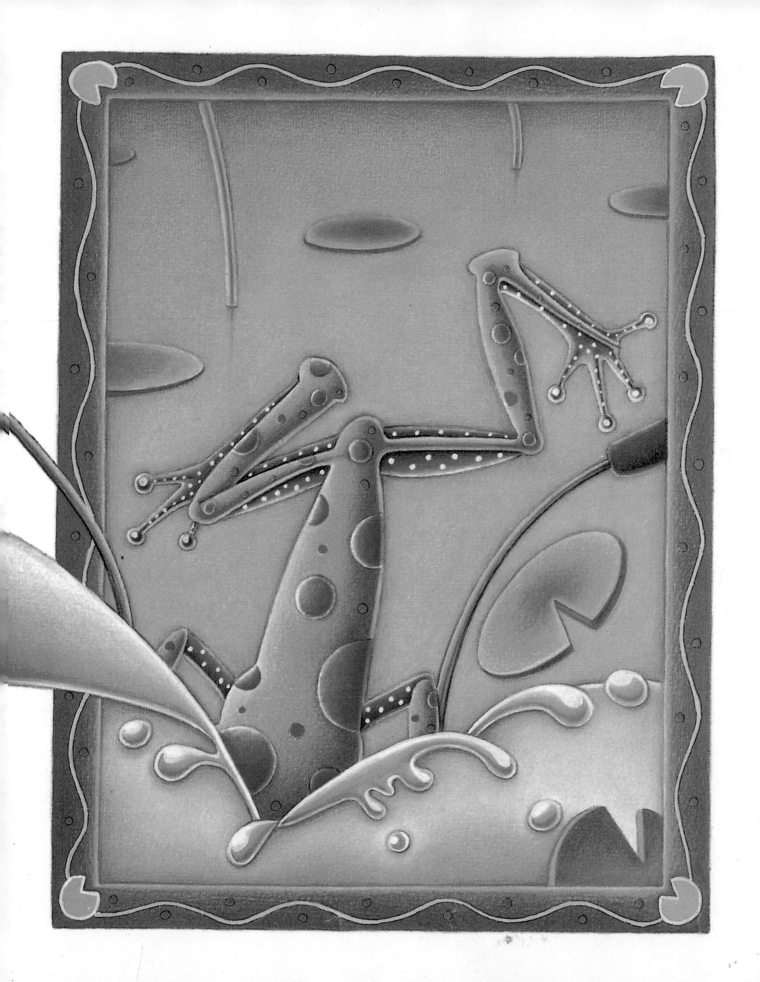

econd, Martí came across a gorilla gathering guavas.

"Excuse me," said Martí, "are those mangos?"

"Of course not," groaned the gorilla. "Mangos are much bigger. These are guavas."

"Thank you," said Martí. He made a note that a mango is a fruit bigger than a guava, and went on.

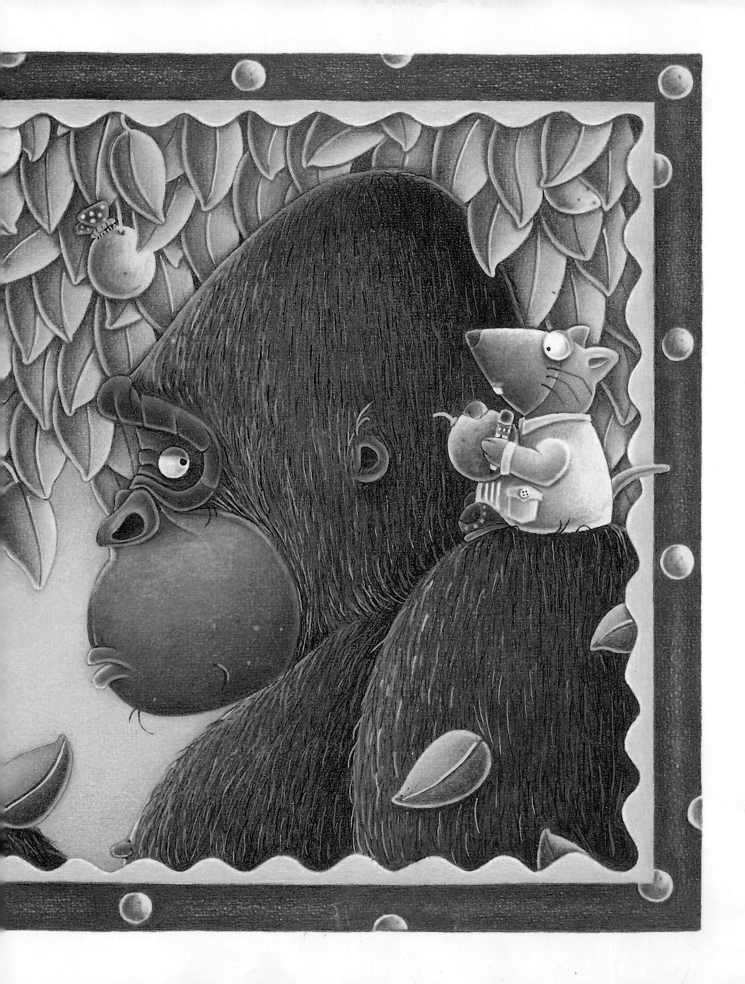

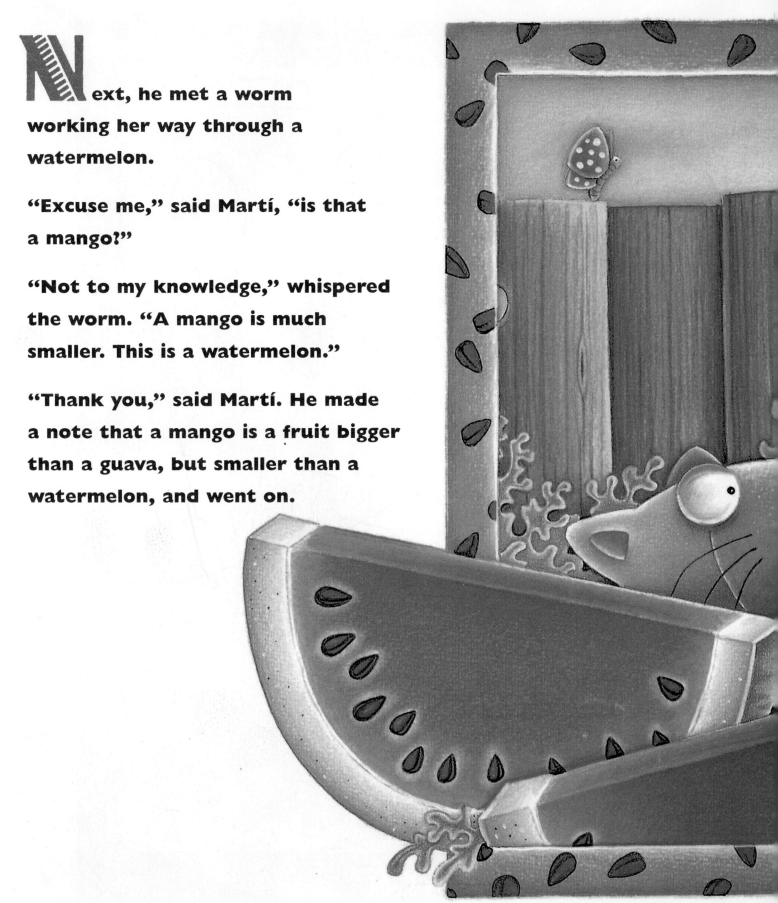

Next, he met a worm working her way through a watermelon.

"Excuse me," said Martí, "is that a mango?"

"Not to my knowledge," whispered the worm. "A mango is much smaller. This is a watermelon."

"Thank you," said Martí. He made a note that a mango is a fruit bigger than a guava, but smaller than a watermelon, and went on.

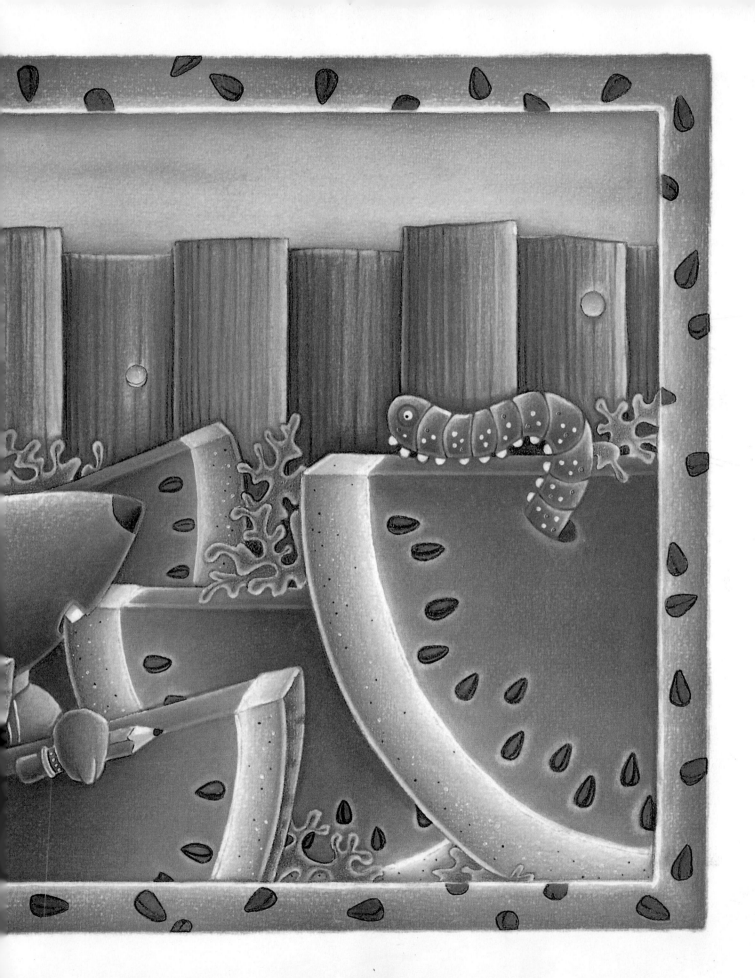

oon after, Martí saw a kangaroo collecting kiwis.

"Excuse me," said Martí, "are those mangos?"

"Not at all," crooned the kangaroo. "Mangos are much smoother. These are kiwis."

"Thank you," said Martí. He made a note that a mango is a fruit bigger than a guava, but smaller than a watermelon, and smoother than a kiwi, and went on.

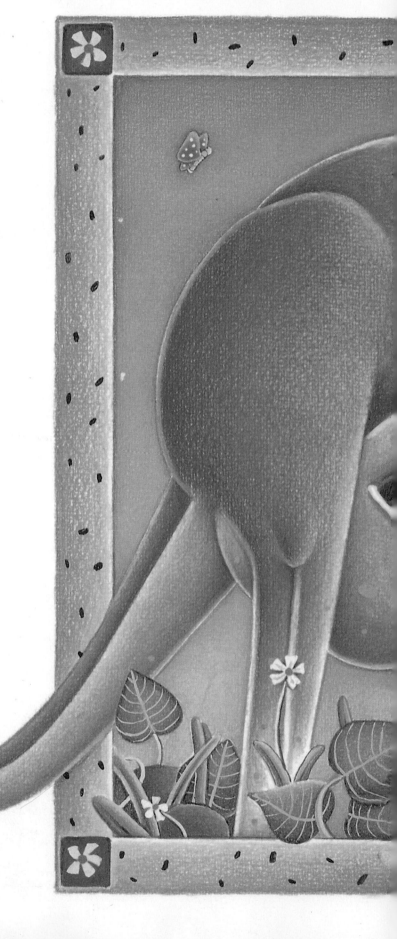

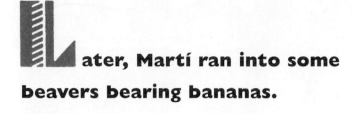Later, Martí ran into some beavers bearing bananas.

"Excuse me," said Martí, "are those mangos?"

"No, no, no," babbled a beaver. "Mangos are much rounder. These are bananas."

"Thank you," said Martí. He made a note that a mango is a fruit bigger than a guava, but smaller than a watermelon, smoother than a kiwi, and rounder than a banana, and went on.

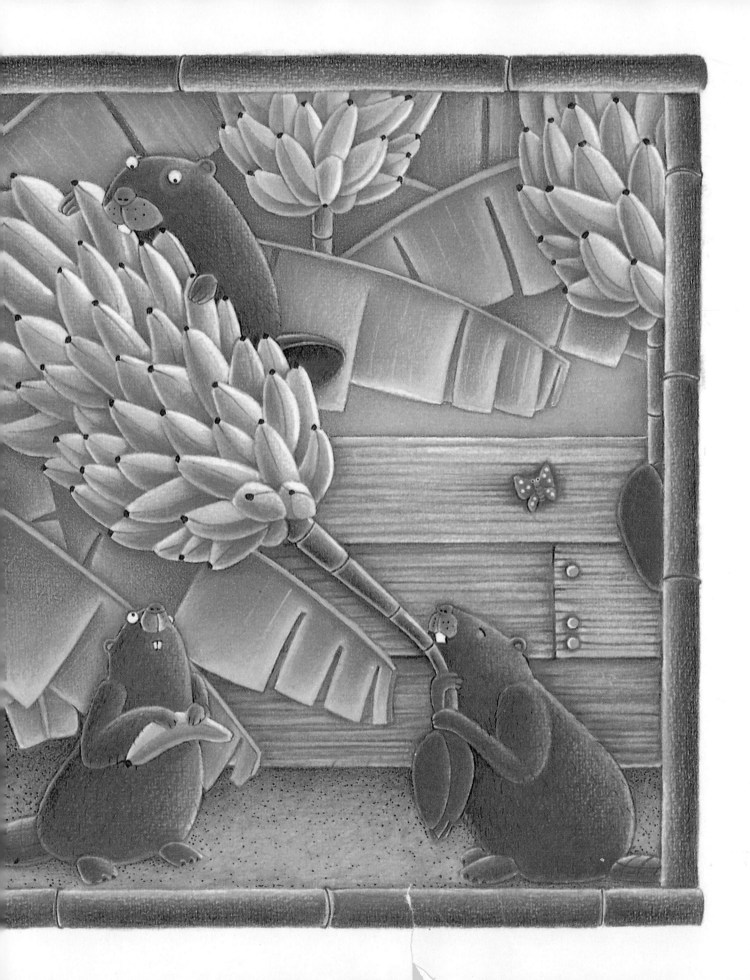

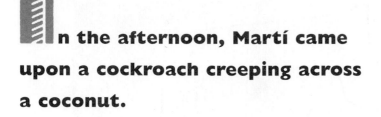In the afternoon, Martí came upon a cockroach creeping across a coconut.

"Excuse me," said Martí, "is that a mango?"

"Hardly!" croaked the cockroach. "A mango is much softer. This is a coconut."

"Thank you," said Martí. He made a note that a mango is a fruit bigger than a guava, but smaller than a watermelon, smoother than a kiwi, rounder than a banana, and softer than a coconut, and went on.

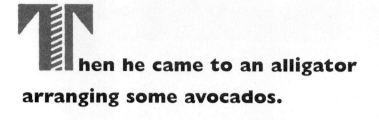

Then he came to an alligator arranging some avocados.

"Excuse me," said Martí, "are those mangos?"

But the alligator did not answer. So Martí went on.

234

By now it was getting late, and Martí had become quite discouraged. He decided to head home without his mango. When he got there, he sat down, tired from his search.

"I'll never find this mango," said Martí unhappily. "I can't find anything. I can't go to Gomez's party without a mango. I'm a failure."

Martí was a very depressed mouse.

ust then Frog came bouncing by on a fig.
"I see you've found your mango," he said to Martí.

"Please don't tease me," begged Martí. "I have
not found my mango."

"But you're sitting right on
it!" bellowed Frog, and he
bounced off down the hill.

239

Martí looked down to see just what it was he was sitting on. "Could this be a mango?" he thought. He referred to his notes.

a mango is a fruit

Bigger than a guava

Smaller than a Watermelon

Smoother than a kiwi

Rounder than a Banana

Softer than a Coconut

"This *is* a mango!" cheered Martí. And he smiled a very big smile.

Martí was a very happy mouse.

240

241

from Fraction Action

A Fair Share

by Loreen Leedy

One Saturday at about noon, Sadie heard a loud knock at the door.

Hello Sadie! Is this a good time for us to drop in?

I was just fixing lunch.

Wonderful! We'll help.

What about this watermelon?

If you cut it into FOURTHS, everybody will get an equal share.

247

THINK ABOUT READING

Answer the questions in this story map.
Write on another sheet of paper.

SETTING

1. Where does the story *Martí and the Mango* take place?

CHARACTERS

2. Who is the main character?

3. Name two other characters in the story.

PROBLEM

4. What does Martí need to find?

5. Why is it hard for Martí to find that?

SOLUTION

6. How does Martí try to solve his problem?

7. Where does Martí finally find a mango?

WRITE NOTES THAT COMPARE

Help Martí find a piece of missing sports equipment. Write one note that tells what the missing thing is. Then write three notes that compare it to other things.

LITERATURE CIRCLE

How are Martí and his friends like Sadie and her friends? How are they different? Which group of characters is more helpful? Why?

Author
Daniel Moreton

The books by Daniel Moreton are fun. They're more than just fun, though. Moreton's stories help readers learn more about Cuba, the country where his family once lived. Moreton says that his character Martí is a Cuban mouse! He lives on a small island, and the country of Cuba is an island. Martí is even named after a famous Cuban hero.

Another Book by Daniel Moreton

- *La Cucaracha Martina: A Caribbean Folktale*

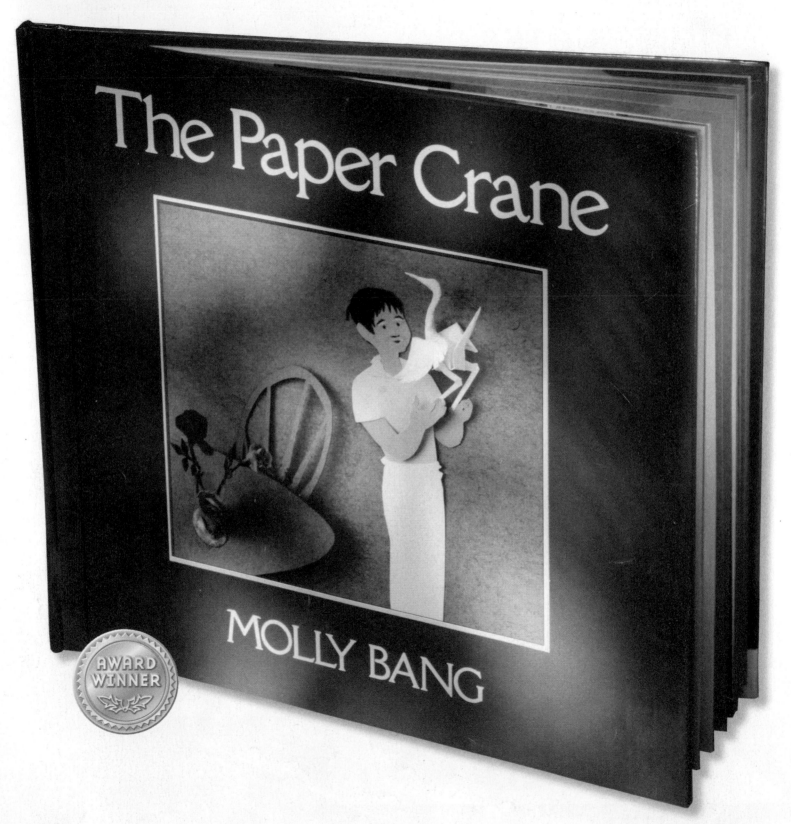

The Paper Crane

MOLLY BANG

AWARD
WINNER

A man once owned a restaurant on a busy road.
He loved to cook good food and he loved to serve it.
He worked from morning until night, and he was happy.

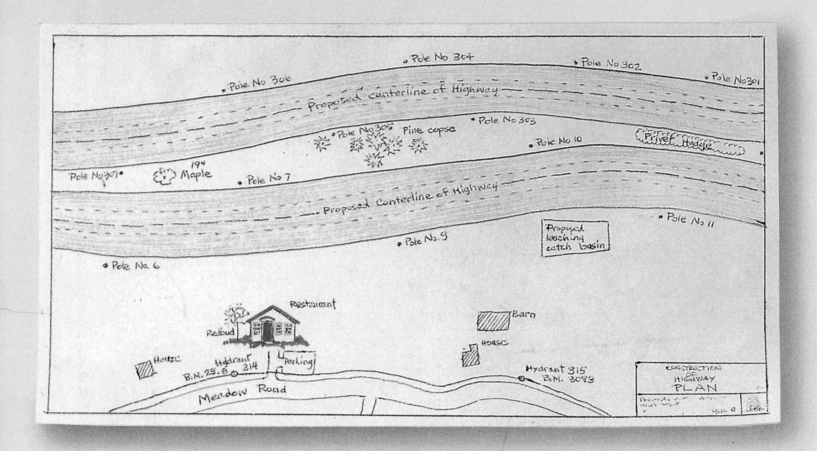

But a new highway was built close by. Travelers drove
straight from one place to another and no longer stopped
at the restaurant. Many days went by when no guests
came at all. The man became very poor, and had nothing
to do but dust and polish his empty plates and tables.

One evening a stranger came into the
restaurant. His clothes were old and worn,
but he had an unusual, gentle manner.

Though he said he had no money to pay for food, the owner invited him to sit down. He cooked the best meal he could make and served him like a king.

When the stranger had finished, he said to his host, "I cannot pay you with money, but I would like to thank you in my own way."

He picked up a paper napkin from the table and folded it into the shape of a crane. "You have only to clap your hands," he said, "and this bird will come to life and dance for you. Take it, and enjoy it while it is with you." With these words the stranger left.

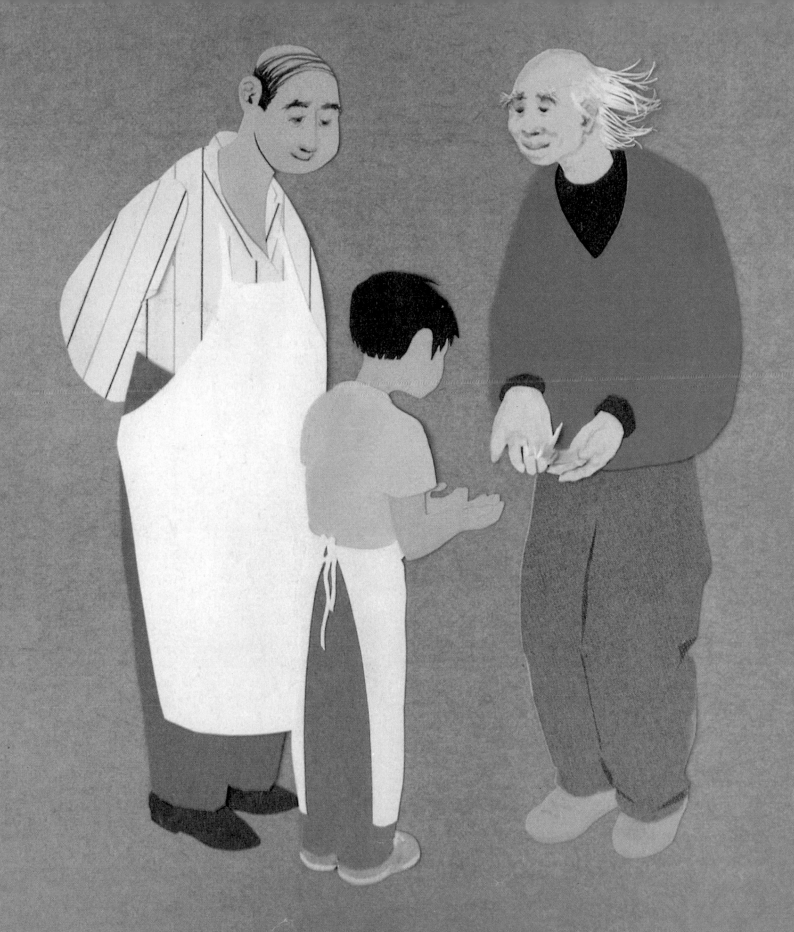

It happened just as the stranger had said. The owner
had only to clap his hands and the paper crane became
a living bird, flew down to the floor, and danced.

Soon word of the dancing crane spread, and people came from far and near to see the magic bird perform. The owner was happy again, for his restaurant was always full of guests.

He cooked and served and had company from morning until night.
The weeks passed.   And the months.

One evening a man came into the restaurant. His clothes were old and worn, but he had an unusual, gentle manner. The owner knew him at once and was overjoyed.

The stranger, however, said nothing. He took a flute from his pocket, raised it to his lips, and began to play.

The crane flew down from its
place on the shelf and danced
as it had never danced before.
The stranger finished playing,
lowered the flute from his lips,
and returned it to his pocket.
He climbed on the back of the
crane, and they flew out of the
door and away.

266

The restaurant still stands by the side of the road, and guests still come to eat the good food and hear the story of the gentle stranger and the magic crane made from a paper napkin. But neither the stranger nor the dancing crane has ever been seen again.

Mary Rodas
Toy Designer

**A toy that's NOT fun?
That's a PROBLEM!**

Some people just love problems! Finding and fixing problems are part of some people's jobs.

Mary Rodas is the vice president of Catco Inc., a toy company. When the company makes a toy, Rodas's job is to look at it and see if there is any problem. She works on the toy to make sure it's fun!

Questions

for Mary Rodas

Here's how toy designer Mary Rodas solves problems on her job.

Q How did you get this job while you were still in school?

A When my neighbor Donald Spector started inventing toys, he would ask me what I thought of his new toy ideas. When he started his own toy company, he hired me to help him.

Q How do you decide if a toy might have a problem?

A First, a designer shows me a drawing of a new toy. Then, I look at a model of it. I try to think if the toy will be fun for children. If not, it should be changed.

Q **Have you solved a problem about a toy?**

A One day I was looking at a white ball called a Balzac Balloon Ball.® I thought the color wasn't exciting, so the designers made the ball in bright colors. Now the ball is a big hit!

®

®

Mary Rodas's Tips
for Solving Problems

1 Be positive. Believe you can solve the problem.

2 Don't give up. Keep trying ways to find a solution.

3 If you need help, don't be afraid to ask for it.

Think About Reading

1. Why does the stranger make a paper crane for the owner of the restaurant?

2. At the beginning of the story, why is the owner of the restaurant happy?

3. Why do you think the paper crane was such a good gift?

4. Look at the picture on page 260. What do you think the boy and the owner might be saying?

5. The restaurant is busy even though the paper crane is gone. Why do you think people come back to the restaurant? Why do you think new people come to the restaurant?

Write an Ad

Help the restaurant owner to bring in even more people to his restaurant. Write an ad the owner could put in the newspaper. In your ad, tell about at least two things that make the restaurant special. You may want to draw a picture as part of your ad.

Literature Circle

What parts of the story could happen in real life? What parts could not happen? What was your favorite part of the story?

Author
MOLLY BANG

Molly Bang grew up with books. In fact, her mother is a writer. Bang has illustrated some of her mother's books.

Molly Bang worked hard to find the best way to make the pictures for *The Paper Crane*. Finally, she decided to cut shapes from colored construction paper. It took her a whole year to make all the pictures for this book!

More Books by
MOLLY BANG

- *Goose*
- *Tye May and the Magic Brush*
- *Common Ground: The Water, Earth, and Air We Share*

Lights! Camera! Action!

Lights! Camera! Action!

THEME

Creative teams produce great performances.

www.scholastic.com

Visit the kids' area of **www.scholastic.com** for the latest news about your favorite Scholastic books. You'll find sneak previews of new books, interviews with authors and illustrators, and lots of other great stuff!

UNIT 3

Welcome to

LITERACY PLACE

Have Fun at a Children's Theater

Creative teams produce great performances.

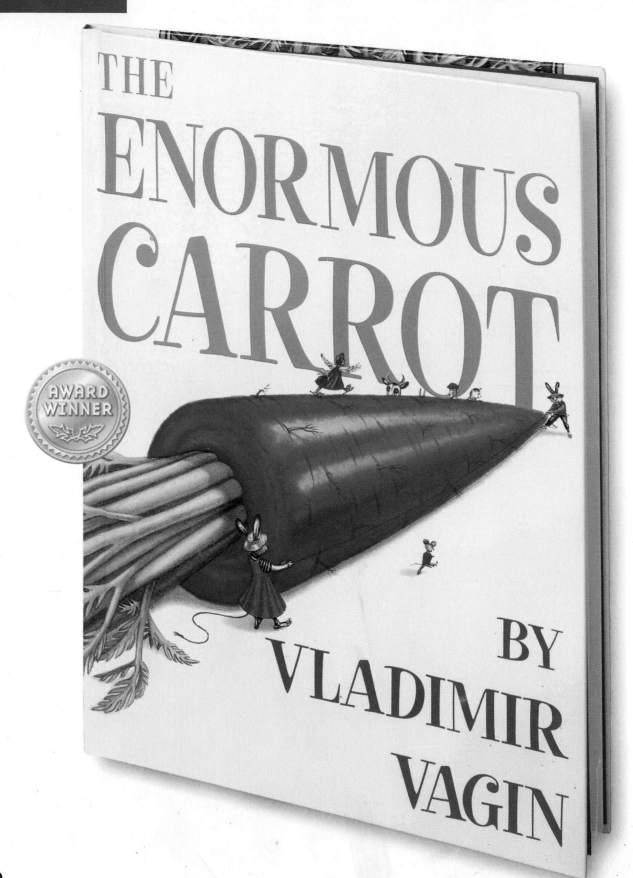

THE ENORMOUS CARROT

AWARD WINNER

BY VLADIMIR VAGIN

Early one spring, Daisy and Floyd planted seeds in their garden.

Each day, they watered and weeded.

Everything grew exactly as they had planned.

Then one morning . . .

Daisy and Floyd discovered an enormous carrot growing in the middle of their garden.

"This carrot is ready to pick," said Floyd.
So Floyd tried to pull the carrot out of the ground.
But the carrot stayed put.
It wouldn't come out.

"I'll pull it out," said Daisy.
Daisy tried to pull the carrot out of the ground.
But the carrot stayed put.
It wouldn't come out.

Then Daisy and Floyd tried together
to pull the carrot out of the ground.

They tugged and they lugged.
But the carrot stayed put. It wouldn't come out.

Just then, their friend Mabel came by.

"Will you help us pull this carrot out?" asked Daisy.
"Naturally," said Mabel.

So Daisy, Floyd, and Mabel tried together
to pull the enormous carrot out of the ground.
They heaved and they ho'd.
But the carrot stayed put. It wouldn't come out.

Just then, their friend Henry came by.
"Will you help us pull this carrot out?" asked Mabel.
"Glad to," said Henry.

So Daisy, Floyd, Mabel, and Henry tried together
to pull the enormous carrot out of the ground.
They grunted and they groaned.
But the carrot stayed put. It wouldn't come out.

294

Just then, their friend Gloria came by.

"Will you help us pull this carrot out?" asked Henry.

"Absolutely," said Gloria.

So Daisy, Floyd, Mabel, Henry, and Gloria tried
together to pull the enormous carrot out of the ground.
They teamed and they towed.
But the carrot stayed put. It wouldn't come out.

296

Just then, their friend Buster came by.
"Will you help us pull this carrot out?" asked Gloria.
"Sure thing," said Buster.

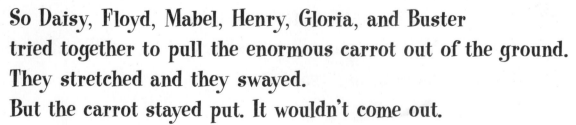

So Daisy, Floyd, Mabel, Henry, Gloria, and Buster
tried together to pull the enormous carrot out of the ground.
They stretched and they swayed.
But the carrot stayed put. It wouldn't come out.

Just then, their friend Claire came by.
"Will you help us pull this carrot out?" asked Buster.
"I'd be delighted," said Claire.

 So Daisy, Floyd, Mabel, Henry, Gloria, Buster, and Claire
tried together to pull the enormous carrot out of the ground.
They hollered and they hauled.
But the carrot stayed put. It wouldn't come out.

Just then, their friend Lester came by.

"May I help you pull that carrot out?" asked Lester.

"You're much too small!" said Claire.

"Let me try," said Lester.

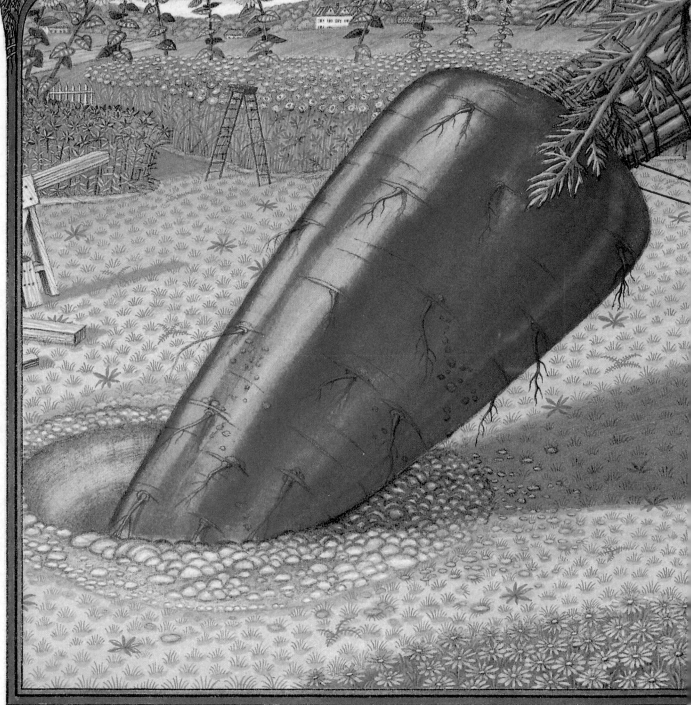

So Daisy, Floyd, Mabel, Henry, Gloria, Buster, Claire, and Lester
tried together to pull the enormous carrot out of the ground.
They tugged and they lugged,
they heaved and they ho'd,
they grunted and they groaned,

they teamed and they towed,
they stretched and they swayed,
they hollered and they hauled,
and all at once . . .

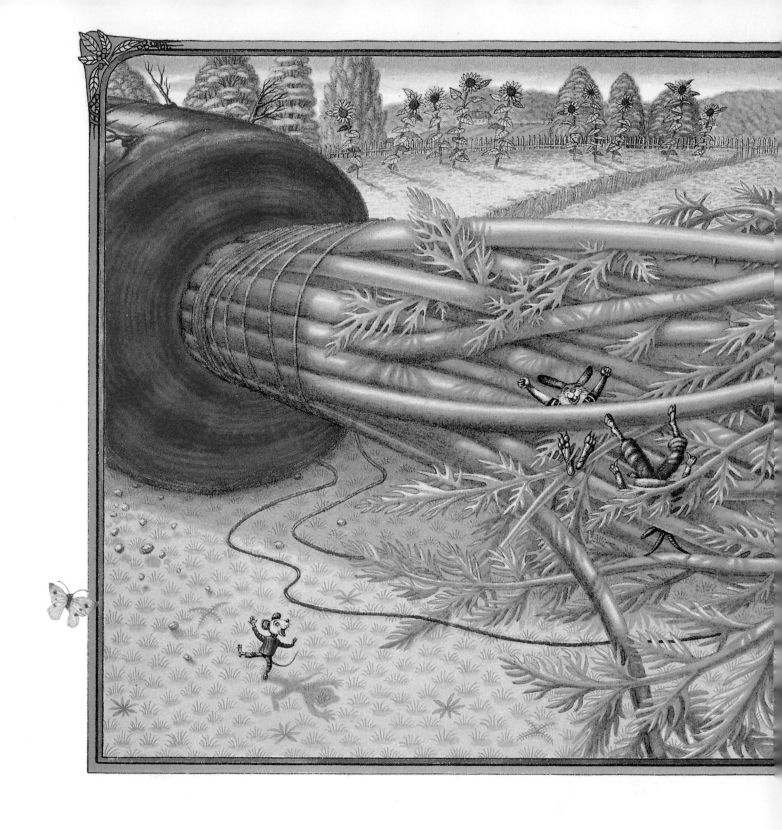

the enormous carrot . . .

CAME OUT!

Then Daisy, Floyd, Mabel, Henry, Gloria, Buster, Claire, Lester, and all

their friends ate every bit of that enormous carrot until it was all gone.

That afternoon, Daisy said, "I can't wait to see what comes up tomorrow."
"Neither can I," said Floyd. "But first it's time for an ENORMOUS REST."

from **Tomie dePaola's Book of Poems**

Celebration

by *Alonzo Lopez*
illustrated by Tomie dePaola

I shall dance tonight.
When the dusk comes crawling.
There will be dancing
   and feasting.
I shall dance with the others
    in circles,
      in leaps,
        in stomps.
Laughter and talk
   will weave into the night,
Among the fires
   of my people.
Games will be played
And I shall be
   a part of it.

Think About Reading

Think about *The Enormous Carrot*. Finish each sentence in the story map. Do your work on another sheet of paper. Draw pictures to go with your sentences.

Setting

1. The story takes place in _____.

Characters

2. The main characters are _____ and _____ and their friends.

Problem

3. Daisy and Floyd grow an enormous carrot, but _____.

Ending

4. Finally, Daisy and Floyd and six of their friends _____.

Write a Sign

Daisy and Floyd's garden has become famous. Everyone wants to come and see their enormous vegetables. Now they need a sign for their garden gate. Write a sign that Daisy and Floyd can place there.

THE CARROT FEAST

Literature Circle

Once you start reading this story, it's hard to stop. Think about the story. What happens that makes you want to keep reading?

Author
Vladimir Vagin

Vladimir Vagin was born in Russia. He grew up not far from Moscow. Then he moved to Moscow, where he became the art director of a large publishing company. Now he lives in the United States. He and Frank Asch have worked together on several books for children. These books are written in English and in Russian, too.

More Books By Vladimir Vagin

- *The Nutcracker Ballet*
- *Here Comes the Cat!* (with Frank Asch)
- *Dear Brother* (with Frank Asch)

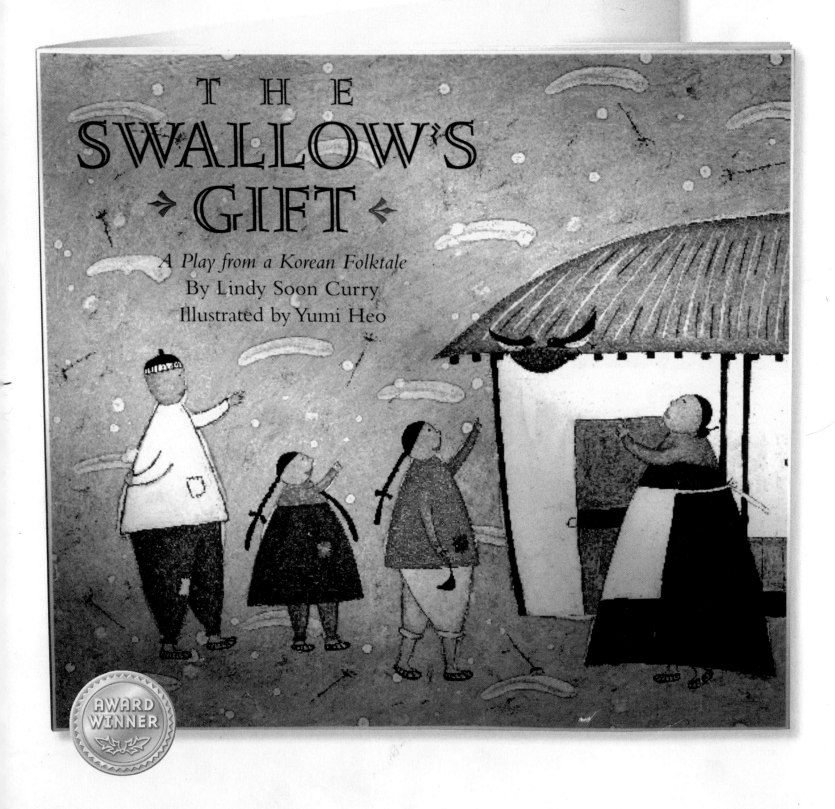

THE
SWALLOW'S
→GIFT←

A Play from a Korean Folktale
By Lindy Soon Curry
Illustrated by Yumi Heo

AWARD WINNER

CHARACTERS

Narrator
Nolbu, selfish older brother
Hungbu, kind younger brother
Mother, wife of Hungbu
Sister, daughter of Hungbu
Brother, son of Hungbu
Swallow

NARRATOR

Long ago in old Korea, two brothers lived together in a large house that their father had built. For many years they got along well. Then one winter day Nolbu got angry and ordered his younger brother Hungbu to move out.

Our play begins as Hungbu and his family set out in search of a new place to live.

SISTER
We have been walking for such a long time.

BROTHER
I'm so cold and tired. Where will we sleep tonight?

HUNGBU
Don't worry children. Here is a shack. You gather leaves and branches. Mother and I will patch the cracks and make the house cozy and warm.

MOTHER
By working together, we'll make it through the winter. But each of us must help.

SISTER
I'll help clean the house.

BROTHER
I'll gather firewood.

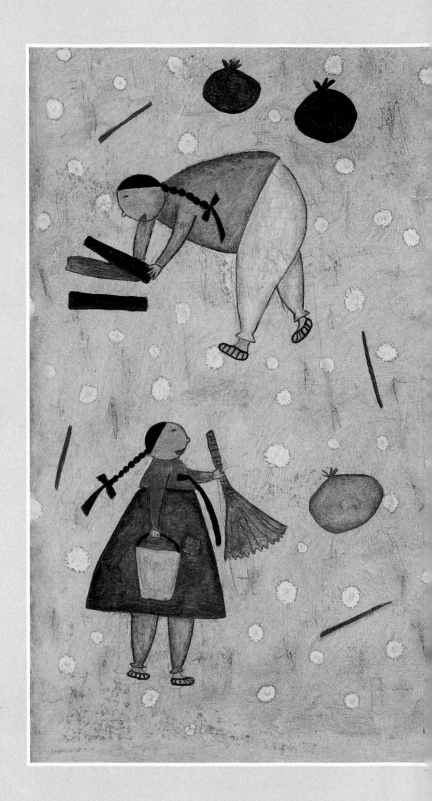

NARRATOR

After a long cold winter, Hungbu and his family were glad to see spring arrive. They planted a garden and watched a pair of swallows build a nest on their roof. One day while they were gardening . . .

BROTHER

Look! This baby swallow fell out of the nest in our roof. I think its leg is broken.

HUNGBU

Baby swallow, don't be afraid. I'll help you. Let me bandage your leg with this cloth.

(He takes a piece of cloth and wraps it around the bird's leg.)

SWALLOW
Thank you. That feels much better.

BROTHER
Here's a bowl of water. Please drink some and get well quickly.

SISTER
Little swallow, eat some sesame seeds. They will make you strong.

SWALLOW
Ah! I feel better already.

MOTHER
You may sleep in this basket until you are strong enough to fly again.

SWALLOW
I'll always remember your kindness.

NARRATOR
The swallow was soon well enough to fly away. But one year later, the little bird returned to thank Hungbu and his family.

BROTHER
Father! There's the swallow with the crooked leg. It's hopping up to you.

HUNGBU
It has a pumpkin seed in its beak.

(He takes the seed from the bird.)

Thank you, swallow.

SWALLOW
This is a gift to thank you for taking care of me.

MOTHER
We'll plant it right away. I'll dig the hole.

SISTER
I'll cover the seed with dirt.

BROTHER
I'll water it and see that it is weeded.

OTHER
see something glittering inside!

UNGBU
old!

STER
ubies!

ROTHER
meralds!

OTHER
et's open the
cond pumpkin.

NARRATOR

That night as the family slept, the swallow's seed sprouted, and it grew and grew. In the morning, Hungbu and his family awoke to an amazing sight.

MOTHER

Look outside! There's a big green plant . . .

SISTER

. . . with three yellow blossoms . . .

BROTHER

. . . that are turning into yellow pumpkins!

(Hungbu goes away and returns with a long saw.)

HUNGBU

Children, if you will help Mother and me,
we can saw through this big pumpkin.

NARRATOR

And so they pushed and pulled and pushed
and pulled until the f   mpkin fell open.

NARRATOR
They pushed and pulled on the saw.

BROTHER
I hear something rattling!

NARRATOR
And the second pumpkin fell open.

HUNGBU
Rice! Thousands of grains of rice!

MOTHER
Now we can eat, eat, eat!

BROTHER
Until our bellies are full, full, full!

SISTER
Let's open the third pumpkin.

NARRATOR
Once again, they pushed and pulled
until the third and last pumpkin
fell open.

MOTHER
Oooh! Yards and yards of silk! Let's
make beautiful clothes and stroll
into town.

NARRATOR
News traveled fast. When Nolbu heard about his brother's good fortune, he went to visit Hungbu.

NOLBU
How did you get all these riches?

HUNGBU
We took care of a swallow with a broken leg. It rewarded us with a seed that grew pumpkins filled with wonderful things. Come live with us, brother. There is plenty for everyone.

NOLBU
No. I'll find my own fortune.

NARRATOR
And Nolbu stormed off to search for a swallow.

NOLBU
Here's a swallow with a crooked leg.

(Nolbu quickly and roughly ties a cloth around the bird's leg.)

NOLBU
Now fly away and bring me back a seed. Make me richer than my brother.

SWALLOW
Ouch, you hurt me! I'll always remember this.

NARRATOR
The following spring, the bird returned to Nolbu and brought him a seed.

SWALLOW
Here's your reward as you wished.

NOLBU
I'll be rich, rich, rich!

NARRATOR

Nolbu planted his seed and it grew just as fast as Hungbu's did, but only two pumpkins sprouted from it instead of three. Nolbu had trouble cutting the pumpkins open because he was all alone. He had no one to help him.

(The first pumpkin breaks open.)

NOLBU

This pumpkin is rotten! It smells terrible! I must open the second one. Perhaps that one will be full of money.

(Nolbu saws the second pumpkin until it falls open.)

NOLBU
Yuck! Spiders and snakes and scorpions! They are crawling over everything! I can't live in this house anymore. Maybe Hungbu will let me live with him after all.

NARRATOR
Nolbu returned to his brother's house and knocked on the door.

HUNGBU

Welcome, brother! Please come in.

NOLBU

I am sorry for the way I treated you. Now my house is full of bugs and snakes. May I live with you?

HUNGBU

Yes, please join us. I'm sorry for what has happened to you.

NOLBU

I'll always work and share equally with you.

HUNGBU

That's the way our father wanted us to live.

NARRATOR

From that day on, the two brothers lived together under the same roof happily ever after.

A Long Ago Look

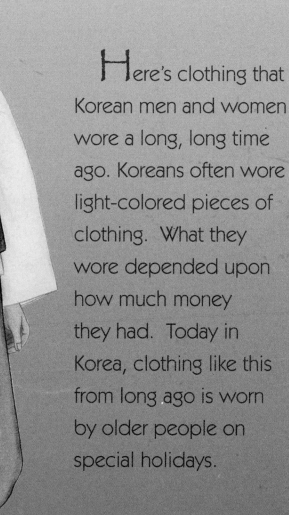

Here's clothing that Korean men and women wore a long, long time ago. Koreans often wore light-colored pieces of clothing. What they wore depended upon how much money they had. Today in Korea, clothing like this from long ago is worn by older people on special holidays.

Think About Reading

1. Why do Hungbu and his family have to find a new home?

2. Why does Nolbu tie a cloth around the sparrow's leg?

3. Why do you think Nolbu has no one to help him cut the pumpkin open?

4. Why do you think Hungbu asks his brother to come and live with him?

5. How are the clothes worn by the characters in *The Swallow's Gift* like the clothes in "A Long Ago Look"?

Write a Description

In the story, Hungbu and his family found riches of gold, rubies, emeralds, rice, and silk in the pumpkins. Suppose the events in *The Swallow's Gift* took place today. What riches might the family find in a pumpkin? Write about your ideas.

Literature Circle

How do the pictures in *The Swallow's Gift* help show that this is an old Korean tale? How would the story of Hungbu and Nolbu be different if it happened now, not long ago? In what ways would it be the same?

Illustrator
Yumi Heo

Yumi Heo remembers hearing the old tale *The Swallow's Gift* when she was a little girl in Korea. She also remembers getting her first box of crayons. She still loves the story, and she still loves making colorful pictures. Now she lives in the United States. She enjoys illustrating books for children. She has started writing books for children, too.

More Books Illustrated by
Yumi Heo

- *A Is for Asia*
- *Father's Rubber Shoes* (She's the author, too.)
- *The Lonely Lioness and the Ostrich Chick: A Masai Tale*

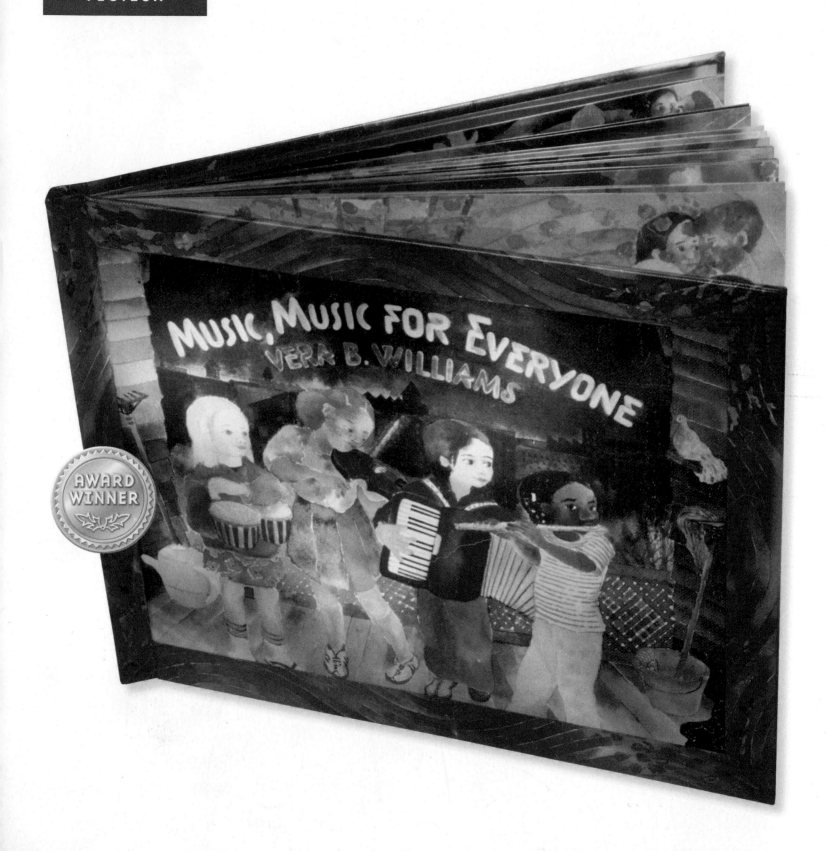

Our big chair often sits in our living room empty now.

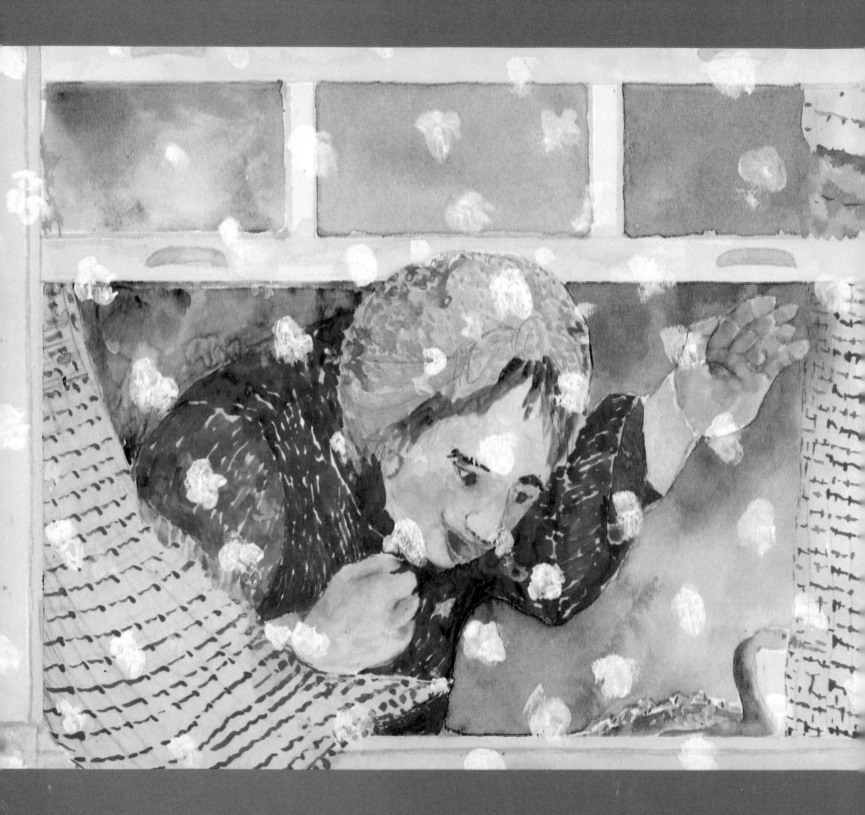

When I first got my accordion, Grandma and Mama used to sit in that chair together to listen to me practice. And every day after school while Mama was at her job at the diner, Grandma would be sitting in the chair by the window. Even if it was snowing big flakes down on her hair, she would lean way out to call, "Hurry up, Pussycat. I've got something nice for you."

But now Grandma is sick. She has to stay upstairs in the big bed in Aunt Ida and Uncle Sandy's extra room. Mama and Aunt Ida and Uncle Sandy and I take turns taking care of her. When I come home from school, I run right upstairs to ask Grandma if she wants anything. I carry up the soup Mama has left for her. I water her plants and report if the Christmas cactus has any flowers yet. Then I sit on her bed and tell her about everything.

Grandma likes it when my friends Leora, Jenny, and Mae come home with me because we play music for her. Leora plays the drums. Mae plays the flute. Jenny plays fiddle and I play my accordion. One time we played a dance for Grandma that we learned in the music club at school.

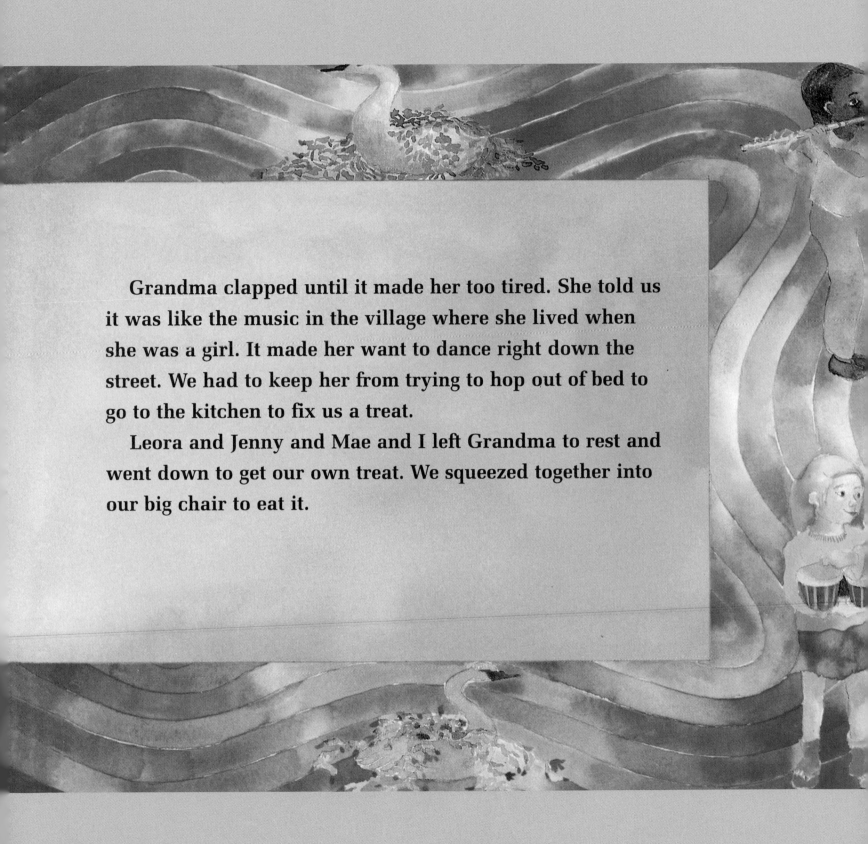

Grandma clapped until it made her too tired. She told us it was like the music in the village where she lived when she was a girl. It made her want to dance right down the street. We had to keep her from trying to hop out of bed to go to the kitchen to fix us a treat.

Leora and Jenny and Mae and I left Grandma to rest and went down to get our own treat. We squeezed together into our big chair to eat it.

"It feels sad down here without your grandma," Leora said. "Even your big money jar up there looks sad and empty."

"Remember how it was full to the top and I couldn't even lift it when we bought the chair for my mother?" I said.

"And remember how it was more than half full when you got your accordion?" Jenny said.

"I bet it's empty now because your mother has to spend all her money to take care of your grandma till she gets better. That's how it was when my father had his accident and couldn't go to work for a long time," Mae said.

Mae had a dime in her pocket and she dropped it into the jar. "That will make it look a little fuller anyway," she said as she went home.

But after Jenny and Leora and Mae went home, our
jar looked even emptier to me. I wondered how we would
ever be able to fill it up again while Grandma was sick.
I wondered when Grandma would be able to come
downstairs again. Even our beautiful chair with roses
all over it seemed empty with just me in the corner of it.
The whole house seemed so empty and so quiet.

342

I got out my accordion and I started to play. The notes sounded beautiful in the empty room. One song that is an old tune sounded so pretty I played it over and over. I remembered what my mother had told me about my other grandma and how she used to play the accordion. Even when she was a girl not much bigger than I, she would get up and play at a party or a wedding so the company could dance and sing. Then people would stamp their feet and yell, "More, more!" When they went home, they would leave money on the table for her.

That's how I got my idea for how I could help fill
up the jar again. I ran right upstairs. "Grandma,"
I whispered. "Grandma?"

"Is that you, Pussycat?" she answered in a sleepy voice.
"I was just having such a nice dream about you. Then I
woke up and heard you playing that beautiful old song.
Come. Sit here and brush my hair."

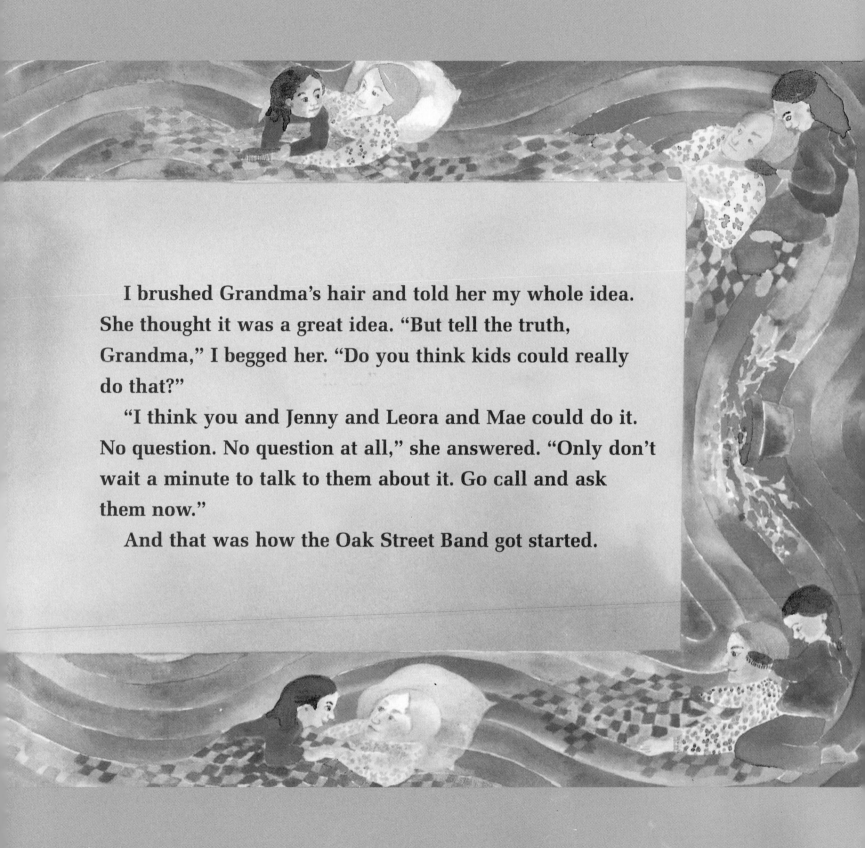

I brushed Grandma's hair and told her my whole idea. She thought it was a great idea. "But tell the truth, Grandma," I begged her. "Do you think kids could really do that?"

"I think you and Jenny and Leora and Mae could do it. No question. No question at all," she answered. "Only don't wait a minute to talk to them about it. Go call and ask them now."

And that was how the Oak Street Band got started.

Our music teachers helped us pick out pieces we could all play together. Aunt Ida, who plays guitar, helped us practice. We practiced on our back porch. One day our neighbor leaned out his window in his pajamas and yelled, "Listen, kids, you sound great but give me a break. I work at night. I've got to get some sleep in the daytime." After that we practiced inside. Grandma said it was helping her get better faster than anything.

At last my accordion teacher said we sounded very good. Uncle Sandy said so too. Aunt Ida and Grandma said we were terrific. Mama said she thought anyone would be glad to have us play for them.

It was Leora's mother who gave us our first job. She asked us to come and play at a party for Leora's great-grandmother and great-grandfather. It was going to be a special anniversary for them. It was fifty years ago on that day they first opened their market on our corner. Now Leora's mother takes care of the market. She always plays the radio loud while she works. But for the party she said there just had to be live music.

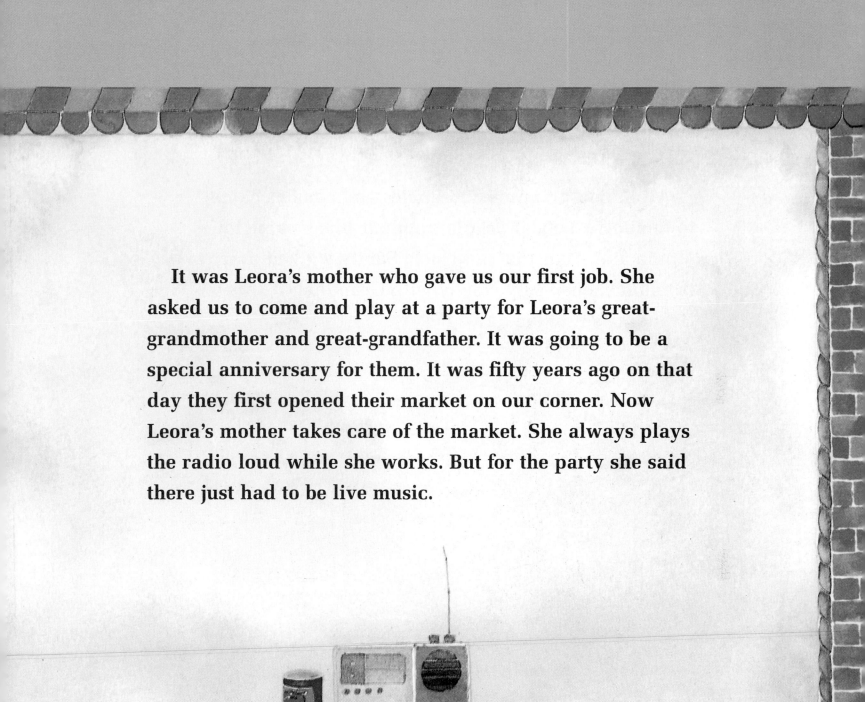

All of Leora's aunts and uncles and cousins came to the party. Lots of people from our block came too. Mama and Aunt Ida and Uncle Sandy walked down from our house very slowly with Grandma. It was Grandma's first big day out.

There was a long table in the backyard made from little tables all pushed together. It was covered with so many big dishes of food you could hardly see the tablecloth. But I was too excited to eat anything.

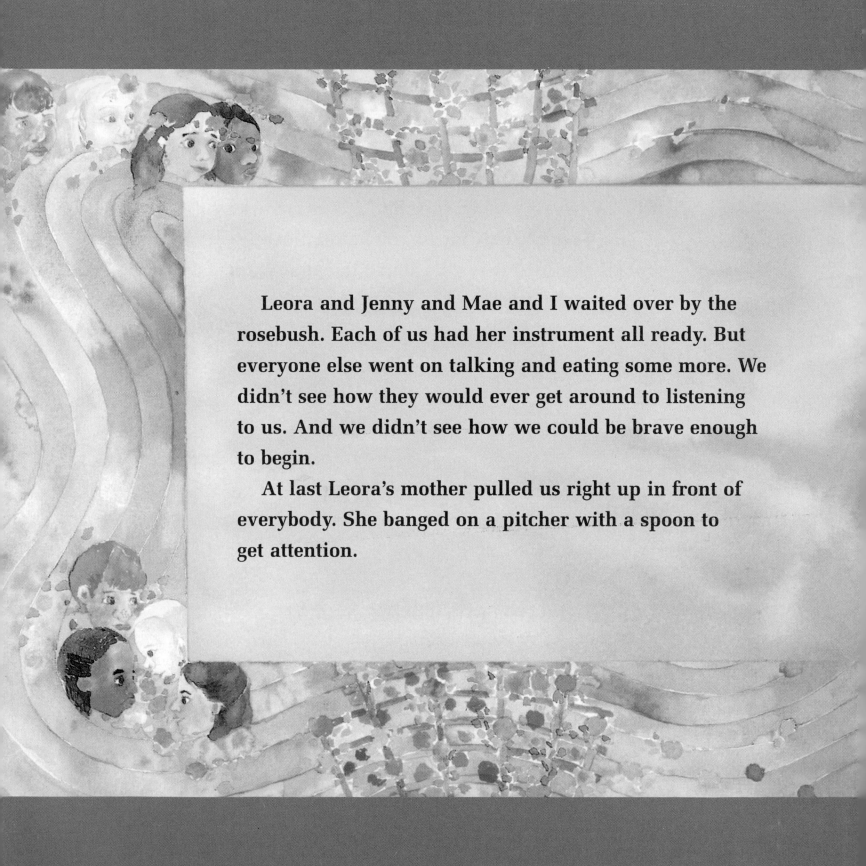

Leora and Jenny and Mae and I waited over by the rosebush. Each of us had her instrument all ready. But everyone else went on talking and eating some more. We didn't see how they would ever get around to listening to us. And we didn't see how we could be brave enough to begin.

At last Leora's mother pulled us right up in front of everybody. She banged on a pitcher with a spoon to get attention.

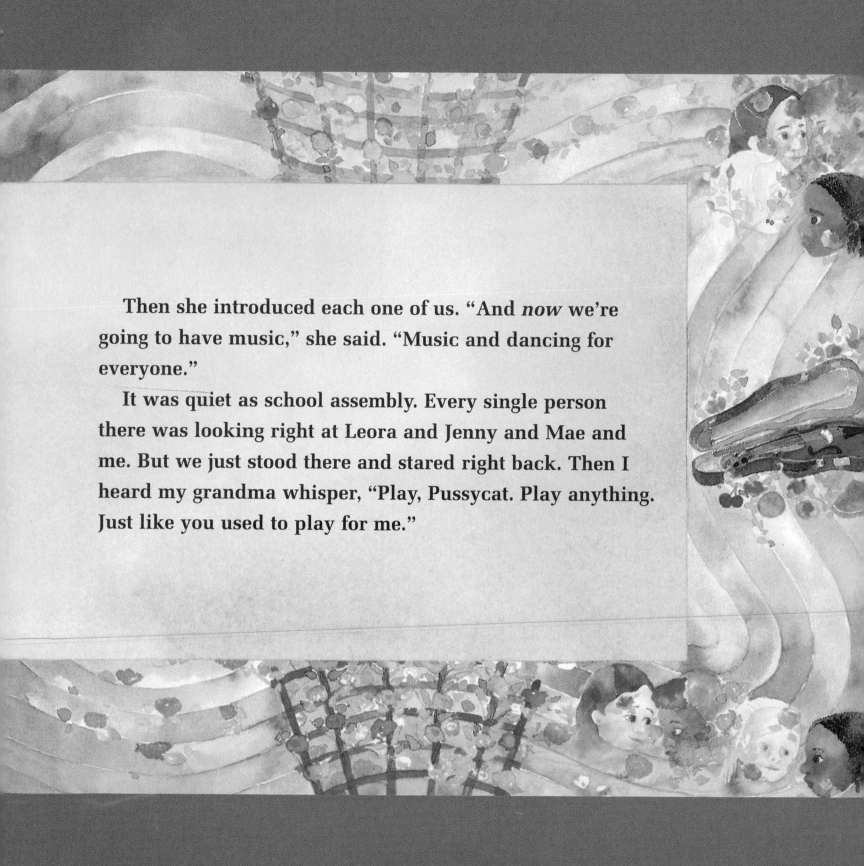

Then she introduced each one of us. "And *now* we're going to have music," she said. "Music and dancing for everyone."

It was quiet as school assembly. Every single person there was looking right at Leora and Jenny and Mae and me. But we just stood there and stared right back. Then I heard my grandma whisper, "Play, Pussycat. Play anything. Just like you used to play for me."

I put my fingers on the keys and buttons of my accordion. Jenny tucked her fiddle under her chin. Mae put her flute to her mouth. Leora held up her drums. After that we played and played. We made mistakes, but we played like a real band. The little lanterns came on. Everyone danced.

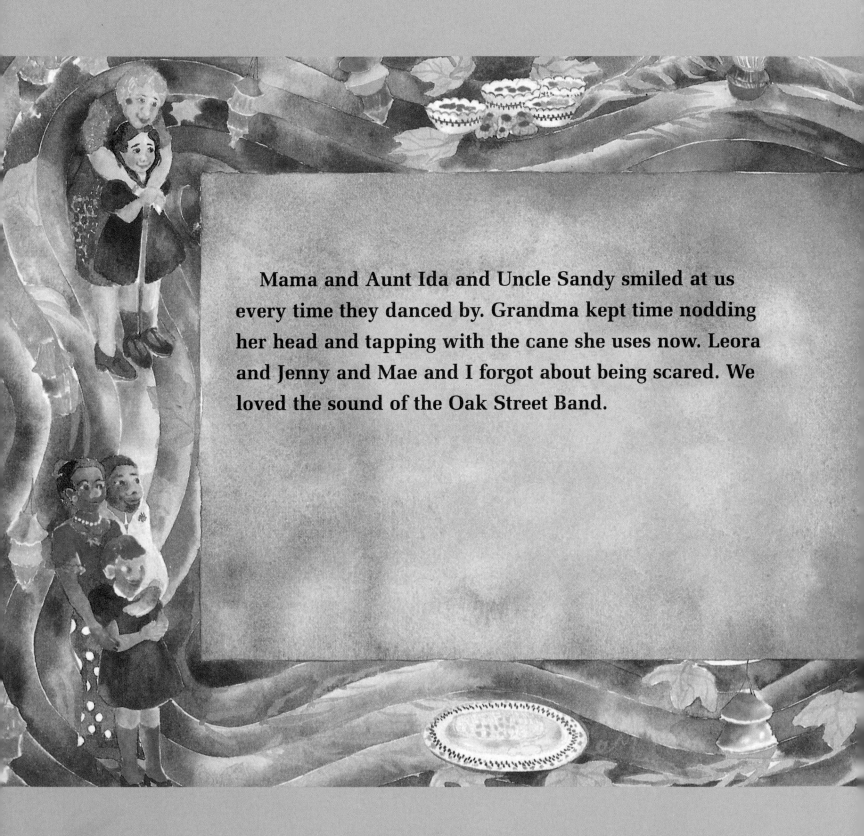

Mama and Aunt Ida and Uncle Sandy smiled at us every time they danced by. Grandma kept time nodding her head and tapping with the cane she uses now. Leora and Jenny and Mae and I forgot about being scared. We loved the sound of the Oak Street Band.

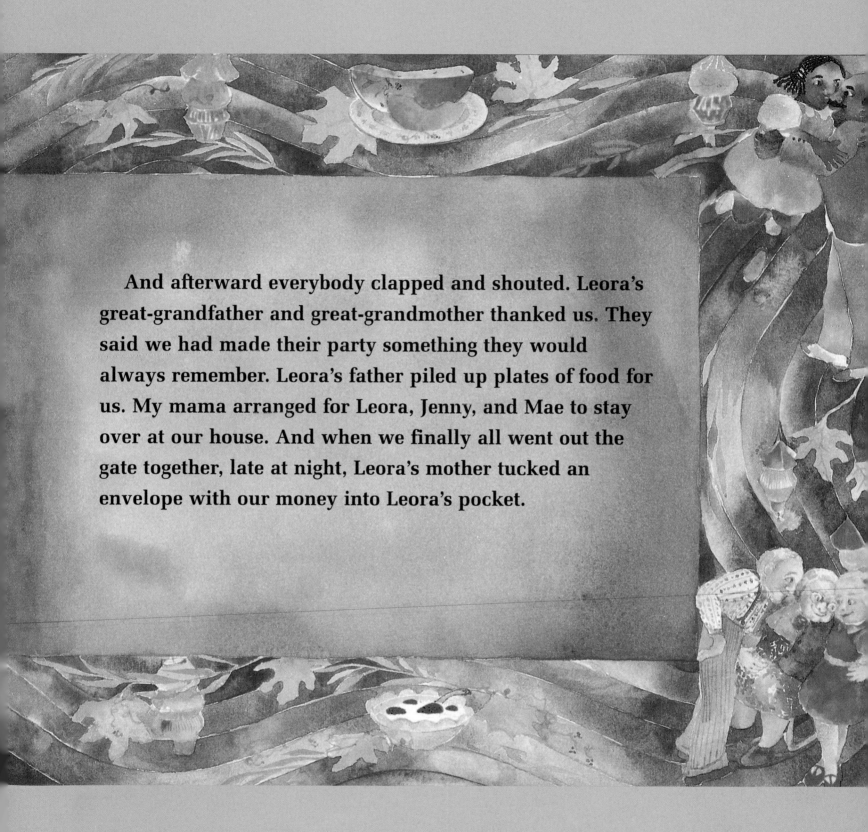

And afterward everybody clapped and shouted. Leora's great-grandfather and great-grandmother thanked us. They said we had made their party something they would always remember. Leora's father piled up plates of food for us. My mama arranged for Leora, Jenny, and Mae to stay over at our house. And when we finally all went out the gate together, late at night, Leora's mother tucked an envelope with our money into Leora's pocket.

As soon as we got home, we piled into my bed to divide the money. We made four equal shares. Leora said she was going to save up for a bigger drum. Mae wasn't sure what she would do with her share. Jenny fell asleep before she could tell us. But I couldn't even lie down until I climbed up and put mine right into our big jar on the shelf near our chair.

Abuelita's Lap

by Pat Mora
Illustrated by Enrique O. Sanchez

I know a place where I can sit
and tell about my day,
tell every color that I saw
from green to cactus gray.

I know a place where I can sit
and hear a favorite beat,
her heart and *cuentos* from the past,
the rhythms honey-sweet.

I know a place where I can sit
and listen to a star,
listen to its silent song
gliding from afar.

I know a place where I can sit
and hear the wind go by,
hearing it spinning round my house,
my whirling lullaby.

Think About Reading

Characters

1. Who is the main character? What does her grandmother call her?

2. Who are the girl's friends?

Problem

3. What does the main character want to do?

4. What group does the girl and her friends form?

Ending

5. How do the girls make money?

Write an Invitation

The girls in the Oak Street Band are going to have a party. They want their friends and family to come and hear their music. Write an invitation they could send. You may add a picture and other designs to your invitation.

Literature Circle

Think about Grandma and Abuelita and what they do and say. How are they alike? How are they different?

Vera B. Williams

Vera B. Williams was in high school when she wrote and illustrated her first book. It was about a giant banana! Most of this author's books are about things that really happened to her. Williams says that the main character in *Music, Music for Everyone* reminds her of herself as a little girl.

More Books by Vera B. Williams

- *Hooray for Me!*
- *Lucky Song*
- *Three Days on a River in a Red Canoe*

The Bremen Town Musicians

by HANS WILHELM

AWARD WINNER

There was once a donkey
whose master made him carry sacks
to the mill year after year.
Now the donkey was getting old,
and his strength began to fail.

When the master realized that the donkey
was of no use to him anymore,
he decided to get rid of him.
But the donkey guessed
that something bad was in the wind,
so he made up his mind to run away.

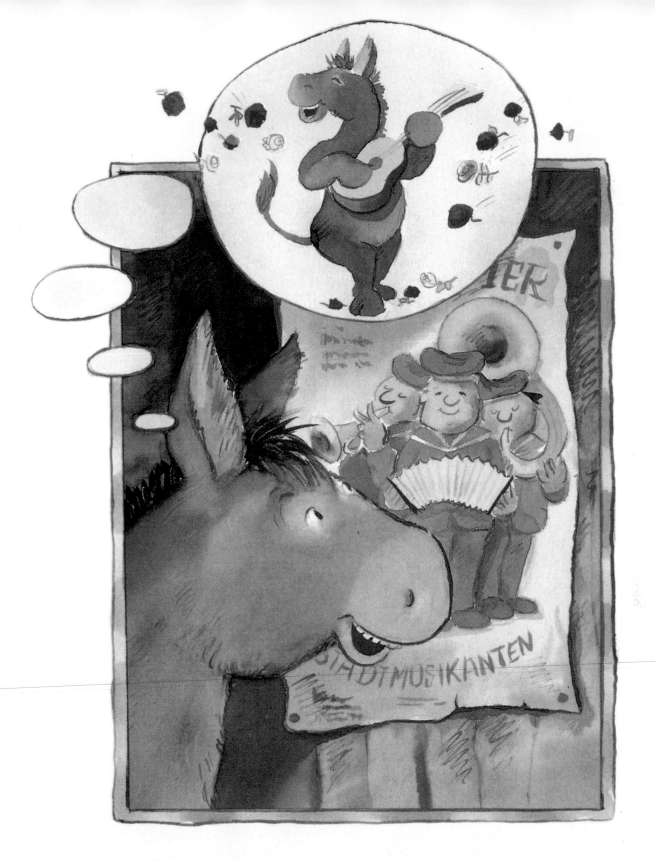

He thought he would take the road to Bremen,
where he might get an engagement as a town musician.

On the way,
he found a dog lying by the side of the road,
panting as if he had been running for a long time.
"Now, Holdfast, why are you so out of breath?"
asked the donkey.

"Oh, dear!" said the dog. "I am old and getting weaker
every day, and I can no longer hunt.
My master was going to kill me, but I escaped!
Now how am I to make a living?"

"I will tell you what," said the donkey.
"I am going to Bremen to become a town musician.
Come with me. I can play the lute,
and you can beat the drum."

The dog liked the idea, and they walked on together.

It was not long before they came to a cat sitting by
the roadside, looking as dismal as three wet days.
"Now then, what is the matter with you, old Whiskerwiper?"
asked the donkey.

"Who can be cheerful when his life is in danger?"
answered the cat. "Now that I am old, my teeth are getting blunt,
and I'd rather sit by the fire than chase after mice.
Because of this, my mistress wanted to drown me,
so I ran away. But now I don't know what is
to become of me."

"Come with us to Bremen," said the donkey,
"and be a town musician. You know how to serenade."

The cat liked the idea and went along with them.

Soon the three runaways passed by a yard.
A rooster was perched on top of the gate,
crowing as loudly as he could.
"Your cries are breaking my heart," said the donkey.
"What is the matter?"

"Tomorrow is Sunday and I have foretold good weather,"
said the rooster, "but my mistress is expecting guests
and has ordered the cook to cut off my head
and put me in the soup.
Therefore, I cry with all my might
while I still can."

"You'd better come along with us, Redhead," the donkey said.
"We are going to Bremen to become town musicians.
We could do with a powerful voice like yours."

This sounded perfect to the rooster, so all four went on together.

But Bremen was too far to be reached in one day.
Towards evening they came to a forest
where they decided to spend the night.

The donkey and the dog lay down under a huge tree,
the cat found a place among the branches,
and the rooster flew up to the top of the tree where he felt safe.
But before he went to sleep, the rooster looked all around
to the four points of the compass.
Suddenly he saw a small light shining in the distance.

He called out to his friends,
"There must be a house over there."

"Let's go and see," said the donkey,
"for this place is not very comfortable."

"And there might be
a few bones," said the dog.

They all set off in the direction of the light.
It grew larger and larger until it led them
to a robber's house, all lighted up.

The donkey—who was the tallest—
went to the window and looked in.
"Well, what do you see?" asked the dog.

"What do I see?" answered the donkey.
"I see a table loaded with wonderful
things to eat and to drink. And
robbers are sitting around the table,
having a great time!"

"That would be perfect for us!"
said the rooster.

"Yes, indeed," replied the donkey.
"I wish we were there."

The four friends put their heads together
to decide how they might scare off the robbers.
Finally they knew what to do.

The donkey placed his forefeet on the windowsill.
The dog got on the donkey's back,
the cat stood on the top of the dog, and lastly,
the rooster flew up and perched
on the cat's head.

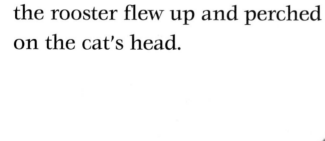

At a given signal, they all
began to perform their music.
The donkey brayed,
the dog barked,
the cat meowed,
and the rooster crowed!

Then they burst into the room,
breaking the windowpanes.
The robbers fled at the dreadful noise.
They thought it was some goblin
and ran to the forest in the utmost terror.

The four friends sat down at the table
and feasted as if they hadn't eaten for weeks.
When they had finished they put out the lights
and looked for places to sleep.
The donkey found a comfortable spot outside,
the dog lay down behind the door,
the cat curled up on the hearth by the warm ashes,
and the rooster settled himself in the loft.
And since they were all very tired from their long journey,
they soon fell asleep.

In the forest, from a safe distance away,
the robbers were watching the house the whole time.
Shortly after midnight they saw that no light was burning
and that everything appeared peaceful.

"We shouldn't have been such cowards and run away!"
said their leader, and he ordered one of them to go back
and check out the house.

The robber went into the house and found everything very quiet.

He went into the kitchen to strike a light, and the cat woke up.
Thinking that the cat's glowing eyes were burning coals,
the robber held a match to them in order to light it.
The cat did not find this funny. He flew into the robber's
face, spitting and scratching.

The robber screamed in terror and ran to get out through the back door. But the dog, who was lying there, leaped up and bit the robber's leg.

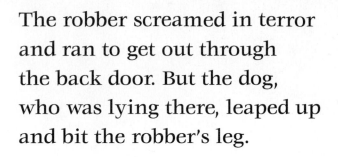

The frightened robber rushed into the yard where the donkey struck out and gave him a great kick with his hind foot.

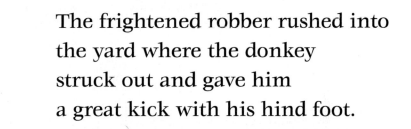

And the rooster, who had been wakened by the noise, cried his loudest, "Kee-ka-ree-kee!"

The robber ran back to the others
as fast as he could,
and said, "Oh, dear!
In that house there is a gruesome witch.
I felt her breath, and she scratched me
with her long nails.
And by the door there stands a monster
who stabbed me in the leg with a knife.
And in the yard there lies a fierce giant
who beat me with a club.
And on the roof
there sits a judge
who cried, 'Bring the thief to me!'
I got out of that place as fast as I could!"

This scared the robbers so much that they never
went back to that house again.

And the four musicians liked their new home
so much that they stayed forever
and never went to Bremen Town at all.

RUBBER GUITAR

Can you make music with rubber bands? By stretching the bands across a baking pan and plucking them, you can mimic the sound of a guitar and learn how string instruments work.

You will need:

Three coloring pens

Baking pan

Rubber bands of varying thickness

1 Stretch the rubber bands lengthwise across the pan.

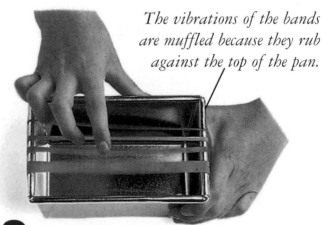

The vibrations of the bands are muffled because they rub against the top of the pan.

2 Pluck the bands. They make a dull sound.

The pens raise the rubber bands above the pan.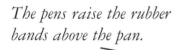

3 Now put a pen underneath the rubber bands at each end of the pan.

The pitch of the notes depends on how fast the bands vibrate. Thin bands vibrate quickly and produce high notes.

4 Pluck the bands again. The sound is much clearer than it was before.

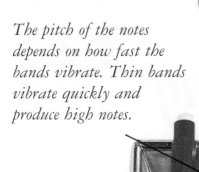

Thick, heavy bands vibrate less quickly and produce low notes.

Vibrations pass through the pens to the pan. Most of the sound comes from the pan as it vibrates.

5 Press the third pen onto the bands. Slide it back and forth while you pluck the bands. The pitch of the notes changes.

The notes get higher as you shorten the vibrating part of each band.

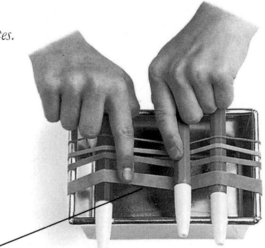

String sounds

Guitar players press the strings with one hand and pluck them with the other. Pressing the strings changes the notes by making the vibrating parts shorter or longer.

Think About Reading

1. What does the donkey want to do in Bremen?

2. When the donkey first meets him, why is the dog out of breath?

3. What were the robbers doing in the house?

4. How would the story be different if the robbers had gone back to the house during the day?

5. Do you think the animals would have had success as musicians in Bremen? Why or why not?

Write a Headline

Everyone is glad that the robbers are gone! In fact, the newspaper is going to print a story about the animals that drove the robbers away. Write a headline for that news story.

Literature Circle

Look at the faces of the robbers. Who do they look like? Why do you think Hans Wilhelm made the robbers look like the animals' masters? What do you think happens to the robbers at the end of the story?

Author
Hans Wilhelm

Hans Wilhelm grew up in Bremen, Germany. Maybe he was close enough to hear the Bremen Town Musicians play!

Wilhelm didn't plan to write and illustrate books. He worked in business for many years. Then he spent three years traveling around the world. After that long trip, he decided to be a writer and illustrator. Now he has written more than 100 books.

More Books by
Hans Wilhelm

- *Don't Cut My Hair!*
- *Bad, Bad Bunny Trouble*
- *The Royal Raven*

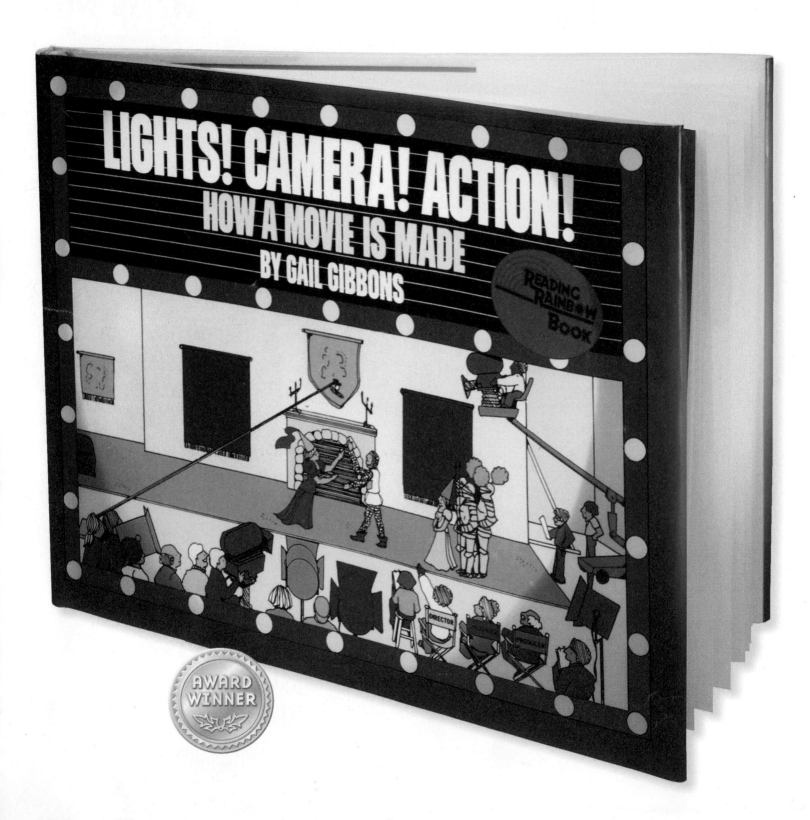

The story is perfect! It is exactly what the
movie producers have been looking for. They
want to take the story and make it into a movie.

The producers hire the people they will need to get started.

It could take millions of dollars to make the movie. The producers describe their project to people who might lend them money. That's how they get their "financial backing."

A major movie studio also likes the project. They will back the movie, too. And when the movie is finished, they will rent out copies to movie theaters.

Step 1: Pre-production...

Now the work begins. The producers hire a scriptwriter. It takes a long time to turn a story into a script, or screenplay. All the dialogue for the actresses and actors is written in the script along with technical directions for lighting, camera angles, and scene changes.

Next, the casting director is hired. She finds actors and actresses to play the leading parts. Sometimes the people chosen are very famous...stars!

There are tryouts for the smaller parts.

The producers need to find just the right locations
for the different scenes. Then the production manager
makes a schedule for filming them.

Sketches are made.

The pre-production crew is bigger now.
The different departments work to get everything
ready. The costume designers, the lighting technicians,

the property department, the set designers,

the sound technicians, and the special effects
department rush to meet the production deadline.

The actresses and actors rehearse...

and rehearse their lines.

Finally, after months of work, everyone and everything is ready. It is time for the different scenes to be filmed.

They will not be shot in the order of the script. All the scenes in the same location, or on the same set, will be shot together. It is easier and costs less that way. When the filming is over, the scenes will be put together in order again.

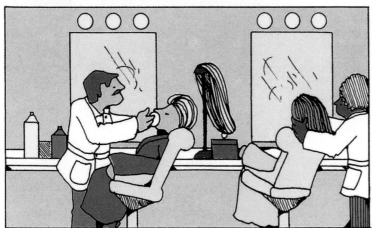

The actresses and actors arrive early each morning.
In the dressing rooms, makeup artists and hair
stylists get them ready for the day's shooting.
Wardrobe assistants help them into their costumes.

Meanwhile, over on the set, the camera operators are in position. The sound technicians are adjusting their equipment. The lighting technicians, called gaffers, have set up the lights.

The actors and actresses come in.

The scene is rehearsed one last time.

Step 2: Production...

Everything looks right.

The director gives a signal. The assistant director yells, "Quiet on the set!"

Production begins.
Lights! Camera! Action!

The director yells, "Cut!" Somebody missed
a line.
They reshoot the scene until it is perfect.
"Print it!" the director yells. He likes the take.

At the end of the day, all the takes are rushed to the film processing lab to be printed.

Each day's film is called a daily. Every morning the producers and director view the dailies from the day before.

Step 3: Post-production...

Once all the scenes have been shot, the film editors take over. They go through the reels and reels of film and select what they need. If it isn't just right, it is out.

The edited film is spliced together in the order of the scenes in the script.

The producers and director view the film. They all agree—it's just what they want. It works!

Dubbing console

Next, music must be added to the sound track.
A composer is hired. The music he creates will set
the mood for the film.

Any mistakes in the dialogue can be corrected now.

Mixers put the music, dialogue, and sound effects
together.

Then the complete sound track will be added to
the film.

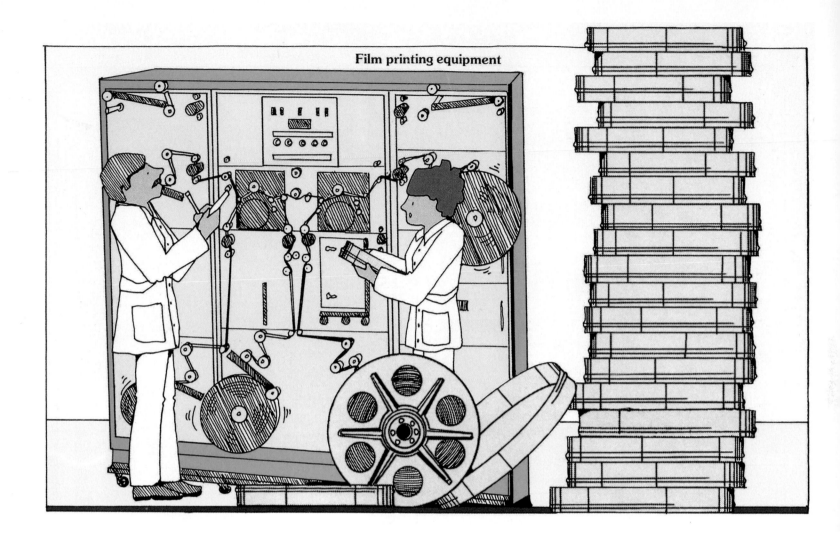

Film printing equipment

The movie is completed.

The first print, called an answer print, is made and given one final check. Then thousands of copies, called release prints, are made.

The movie studio will rent out these copies to the movie theaters. For months, the studio has been advertising the movie and stirring up interest with a big publicity campaign.

The premier showing is held at a big city theater. The
stars are there. All the people who made the movie are
there, too.

Fans and movie critics come to the glamorous event.

The audience waits.

The lights go out and the movie begins.

Judith Martin

Theater Director

Curtain up!
On with the show!

Would you wear a costume made from paper bags? The Paper Bag Players do! They are a theater company that creates plays for children. They really do make their costumes from paper and cardboard.

Before children come to see a play, Judith Martin, the director, has a lot of work to do.

Questions

for Judith Martin

Here's how director Judith Martin works with her team to put on plays.

Q **How do you get your ideas for plays?**

A I try to think about what would make children laugh and what they would really like to see. Sometimes I go to schools and do theater with the children. They have many ideas about what makes a good play.

Q **What happens after you decide on an idea?**

A I write the script with all the lines that the actors will say. They practice their lines while I watch.

422

Q Who else works on the play?

A While the actors are practicing, our artist makes the props—all from paper or cardboard. I also tell her what kinds of costumes the actors need. Our musician writes and plays the music for the show and teaches it to the actors.

Q What's the day of the first performance like?

A The actors look great in their costumes. They know their lines and the music. And now it's the audience's turn to be part of the team. At some point in the play, the children are invited to join in somehow—maybe to dance!

Judith Martin's Tips for Young Directors

1 Work with your group to find a good story or write one about something funny that really happened.

2 Use homemade or old clothes for costumes.

3 Clear part of a room for a stage, and set up chairs for your audience.

THINK ABOUT READING

1. Who turns a story into a script, or screenplay?

2. Why is each scene shot more than once?

3. Why do the producers and director view the dailies from the day before every morning?

4. Why is the sound track important to a film?

5. How is Judith Martin's job different from a movie director's job?

WRITE A POSTER

One way to advertise a movie is to put up posters. Write your own poster for the movie in *Lights! Camera! Action!* Draw a picture for the poster, too.

LITERATURE CIRCLE

Think about all the jobs involved in making a movie or play. Which job would you like to have? Why? Talk about your ideas.

AUTHOR
GAIL GIBBONS

Gail Gibbons loves facts! That's why she writes nonfiction books, not stories. Before she starts writing a book, she collects lots of facts—many more than she can use. She finds many facts in books. She always talks to experts, too. Gibbons spends a lot of time collecting facts for every book, so she only writes about subjects she really likes.

MORE BOOKS BY GAIL GIBBONS

- *Sun Up, Sun Down*
- *Beacons of Light: Lighthouses*
- *Catch the Wind! All About Kites*

GLOS

You will find all your vocabulary words in ABC order in the Glossary. This page shows you how to use it.

This is the **word** you look up. It is the **entry word.**

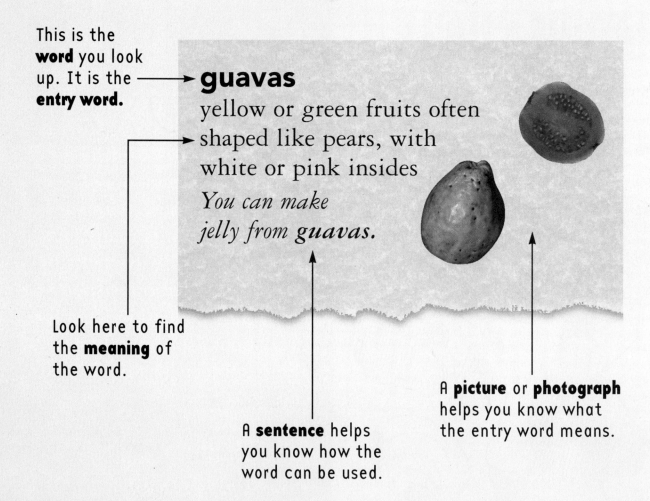

guavas
yellow or green fruits often shaped like pears, with white or pink insides
You can make jelly from guavas.

Look here to find the **meaning** of the word.

A **sentence** helps you know how the word can be used.

A **picture** or **photograph** helps you know what the entry word means.

accordion

a musical instrument with a keyboard played with one hand and a bellows pushed in and out with the other hand

*She played a tune on her **accordion**.*

accordion

actors

people who perform in plays, movies, or TV stories

*The **actors** in this movie are very good.*

actresses

women or girls who perform in plays, movies, or TV stories

*We need three more **actresses** for our school play.*

agreed

said yes to something

*Mom **agreed** to take us to the movies.*

announced

said or told

*He **announced** the date of the play.*

artist

a person who creates

*The **artist** painted a picture of our school.*

assistants

helpers

*On busy days the doctor has two **assistants** in her office.*

avocados

fruits shaped like pears, but with green or black skin and yellow-green insides

avocado

*I like salad with **avocados**.*

bobbed

moved up and down on water

*The swimmers **bobbed** in the waves.*

breeze

a gentle wind

*The **breeze** carried the kite into the sky.*

bubbles

small shiny balls of gas that rise to the surface of liquid

*I blew **bubbles** in my milk with a straw.*

buried

put in the earth or sea

*The dog **buried** a bone in the garden.*

camera

a kind of box used to take pictures or movies

*My **camera** takes very good pictures.*

camera

clothes

things that we wear

*Jamal's favorite **clothes** are a blue T-shirt and jeans.*

clutched

held tightly

*She **clutched** the ball when she caught it.*

company

one or more guests

*Our **company** came at noon for lunch.*

composer

a person who makes up music

*The **composer** sat at the piano to play his new song.*

cowards

people who are afraid of anything that is dangerous or hard to do

*They felt like **cowards** for not climbing all the way to the top.*

danger

something that could hurt you

*The cat escaped **danger** by running up the tree.*

decided

chose after thinking about something

*The class **decided** to present a play to the whole school.*

director

the person who tells the actors what to do in a movie or play

*The **director** told the actor to speak louder.*

dreadful

scary, terrible

*We stayed inside until the **dreadful** storm was over.*

drifting

being carried along by water or air

*The log was **drifting** down the river.*

drum

drums

musical instruments played by beating with sticks

*We listened to the musician play her **drums**.*

emeralds

bright green jewels or the stones they are made from

emerald

***Emeralds** are worth a lot of money.*

fiddle

a musical instrument played by moving a bow across the strings

*He picked up the bow to play his **fiddle**.*

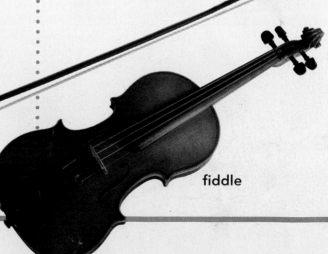

fiddle

fierce

wild and dangerous

*Angry animals are sometimes **fierce**.*

float

to rest on top of water

*A beach ball will **float**, but a baseball will sink.*

flute

a long, thin musical instrument played by blowing through one end and placing fingers over the holes

*Flora played her **flute** for the class.*

flute

fortune

a lot of money

*The prize of $100 seemed like a **fortune** to him.*

garden

a place where people grow flowers, vegetables, or trees

*Let's plant corn in our **garden**.*

gold

a yellow metal

*The coins were made of **gold**.*

gold

grew

got bigger in size

*Grandpa's pine tree **grew** taller every year.*

ground

the surface of the earth; soil

*After the storm, the **ground** was wet.*

growing

getting bigger in size

*My bean plants have been **growing** all summer.*

gruesome

scary and horrible

*He wrote a story about a **gruesome** beast.*

guavas

yellow or green fruits often shaped like pears, with white or pink insides

*You can make jelly from **guavas**.*

guavas

guests

people who are visiting someone's home or staying at a hotel

*Ryan and his brother are **guests** at our house this weekend.*

guitar

a musical instrument played by moving the fingers across the strings

*Our teacher played the **guitar** and sang.*

guitar

helmet

a hard hat that protects the head

*Sam's **helmet** protects his head when he rides his bike.*

helmet

hobby

something that a person does just for fun

*Grandpa's **hobby** is collecting stamps.*

host

a person who greets people in a restaurant

*The **host** seated us at a table near the window.*

idea

a thought

*I have an **idea** for something to do Saturday afternoon.*

imagination

the act of creating pictures in your mind

*Min uses her **imagination** to write stories.*

instrument

something used to make music

The piano is my favorite instrument.

kindness

being nice and helpful to others

The older woman is loved by all for her kindness.

kiwis

small fruits shaped like eggs, with brown fuzzy skin and green insides

We peeled the kiwis and added them to the fruit salad.

kiwis

lake

a big body of fresh water surrounded by land

We skate on the lake when it freezes in winter.

mango

a fruit that has tough skin with a rosy tint and orange insides

A mango is a juicy fruit.

mast

a tall pole on a boat that supports its sails

A sailboat needs a strong mast in a storm.

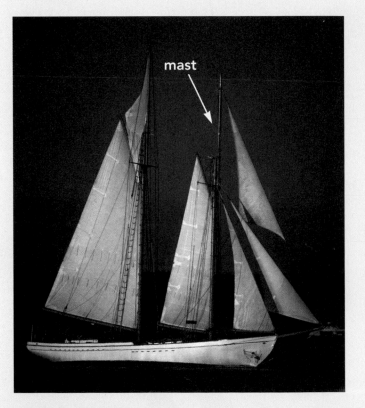

mast

modeled

showed

My friend modeled the way to make a kite.

murmured

spoke in a low, soft voice

*He **murmured** that he didn't like his lunch.*

mystery

something that is not known or is secret

*We solved the **mystery** of the lost money by finding the hole in the bag.*

ocean

the entire body of saltwater covering over half of the earth's surface

*The **ocean** is bigger than any lake.*

overboard

over the side of a boat

*The sailor who fell **overboard** was rescued from the sea.*

photographer

a person who takes pictures with a camera

*A **photographer** took a picture of my class.*

pigsty

a messy, dirty place like a pen for pigs

*Mom called the messy room a **pigsty**.*

planted

put a plant or a seed in the ground to make it grow

*The farmer **planted** wheat in his field.*

polished

made bright and shiny

*Pedro **polished** his shoes until they shined.*

practice

to do something again and again

*We **practice** for the class play every day.*

producers

people who get a movie, show, or play ready to be seen

***Producers** hire the actors, writers, and directors for the movies.*

rowboat

recited
said out loud in front of a group

*He **recited** his poem for the whole class.*

restaurant
a place where people buy and eat meals

*Our family ate dinner at that **restaurant**.*

rewarded
having received money or treats for good work or kind acts

*The girl who found the puppy was **rewarded** with ten dollars.*

riches
money, and things that are worth a lot of money

*The king in the story had jewels and other **riches**.*

ripples
very tiny waves

*The pebble made **ripples** when I threw it in the pond.*

rowboat
a small boat moved through water by using oars

*A **rowboat** has no engine or sail.*

rubies
bright red jewels

*The **rubies** in her necklace were beautiful.*

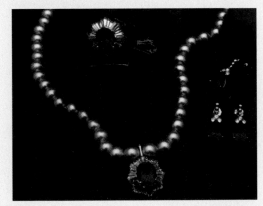

rubies

sail
to glide or move smoothly over water

*Let's watch the ship **sail** across the bay.*

scared

afraid, frightened

*The silly dog was scared of
its shadow.*

scoured

cleaned by rubbing with something
rough

*I scoured the pan with a soap pad
to get it clean.*

scribbled

wrote quickly or without care

*She scribbled a note before she
rushed out of the house.*

scrubbed

cleaned by rubbing hard

*I scrubbed the bathtub with
a soapy brush.*

secret

kept hidden or known by few people

*I keep my journal in a secret
hiding place.*

seeds

small parts of plants from which
new plants can grow

*Those tall flowers began as
tiny seeds.*

seeds

shark

a large fish with sharp teeth that
eats meat

*A shark will catch and eat
other fish.*

shark

sneaker

a soft shoe with a rubber bottom

*The laces on one **sneaker** came untied.*

sneaker

solve

to find the answer

*Can you **solve** this puzzle?*

stranger

someone you don't know

*The man with my uncle was a **stranger** to me.*

surface

the top part or outside layer

*Boats sail on the **surface** of the water.*

swept

cleaned with a broom

*I **swept** all the broken pieces off the floor.*

swish

to move with a soft rustling sound

*Run your fingers through water to hear it **swish**.*

technicians

people who can use or fix machines

*The **technicians** were taking care of the sound at a music show.*

terror

strong fear

*In the story, the mouse ran in **terror** from the cat.*

tiptoed

walked on the toes

*She **tiptoed** quietly down the hall.*

travelers

people who visit another place

*The **travelers** are tired from their long trip.*

treasure

treasure

money, jewels, or other things
of great value

*We read a story about finding
lost **treasure**.*

watered

poured water over something

*She **watered** the grass with a hose.*

watermelon

a large fruit with green skin and
red insides

*We cut the huge **watermelon** into
thick slices.*

watermelon

waves

moving ridges on the surface
of water

*Listen to the **waves** crashing on
the shore.*

waves

weeded

pulled unwanted plants out
of the ground

*Dad **weeded** the yard to make it
look neat.*

whispered

spoke very softly

*He **whispered** because the baby
was sleeping.*

wise

makes good decisions, knows a lot

*Our grandmother is very **wise**.*

Acknowledgments

Grateful acknowledgment is made to the following sources for permission to reprint from previously published material. The publisher has made diligent efforts to trace the ownership of all copyrighted material in this volume and believes that all necessary permissions have been secured. If any errors or omissions have inadvertently been made, proper corrections will gladly be made in future editions.

Unit 2 *Super Solvers* Table of Contents: From THE PAPER CRANE by Molly Bang. Copyright © 1985 by Molly Garrett Bang. Reprinted by permission of Greenwillow Books, a division of William Morrow & Company, Inc.

Unit 1 *Snapshots* Table of Contents: From RONALD MORGAN GOES TO BAT by Patricia Reilly Giff, illustrated by Susanna Natti. Illustrations copyright © 1998 by Susanna Natti. Reprinted by permission of Viking Penguin, a division of Penguin Putnam Inc.

Unit 3 *Lights! Camera! Action!* Table of Contents: From THE ENORMOUS CARROT by Vladimir Vagin. Copyright © 1998 by Vladimir Vagin. Reprinted by permission of Scholastic Inc.

Unit 1 *Snapshots*: "Ducky" from DUCKY by Eve Bunting, illustrated by David Wisniewski. Text copyright © 1997 by Eve Bunting. Illustrations copyright © 1997 by David Wisniewski. Reprinted by permission of Clarion Books/Houghton Mifflin Company. All rights reserved.

"Ronald Morgan Goes to Bat" from RONALD MORGAN GOES TO BAT by Patricia Reilly Giff, illustrated by Susanna Natti. Text copyright © 1988 by Patricia Reilly Giff. Illustrations copyright © 1988 by Susanna Natti. Reprinted by permission of Viking Penguin, a division of Penguin Putnam Inc.

"Baseball Greats":TM/© 1988 Family of Babe Ruth and the Babe Ruth Baseball League, Inc. under license authorized by CMG Worldwide Inc., Indianapolis, IN 46256, www.baberuth.com. The Texas Rangers and New York Yankees insignias depicted in this publication are reproduced with the permission of Major League Baseball Properties, are the exclusive property of the Texas Rangers and the New York Yankees, and may not be reproduced without their written consent. UPPER DECK and the Upper Deck logo are trademarks of The Upper Deck Company, LLC. © 1998 The Upper Deck Company, LLC. Major League Baseball trademarks and copyrights used with permission of Major League Baseball Properties, Inc. All rights reserved. Used with permission.

"Ruby the Copycat" from RUBY THE COPYCAT by Peggy Rathman. Copyright © 1991 by Margaret Rathman. Reprinted by permission of Scholastic Inc.

"I Can" by Mari Evans from PASS IT ON: AFRICAN AMERICAN POETRY FOR CHILDREN by Wade Hudson and Cheryl Hudson. Reprinted by permission of the author. Illustrations copyright © 1993 by Floyd Cooper. Published by Scholastic Inc. by arrangement with Just Us Books.

"Shipwreck Saturday" from SHIPWRECK SATURDAY by Bill Cosby, illustrated by Varnette P. Honeywood. Copyright © 1998 by Bill Cosby. Reprinted by permission of Scholastic Inc.

"Go Fly A Kite" kite design from KITEWORKS by Maxwell Eden. Copyright © 1989 by Maxwell Eden. Reprinted by permission of Sterling Publishing Co., Inc., 387 Park Avenue South, New York, NY 10016.

"George Ancona: Then & Now" from GEORGE ANCONA by George Ancona. Copyright © 1996 by Scholastic Inc.

Unit 2 *Super Solvers*: "Belling the Cat" from ONCE IN A WOOD, adapted and illustrated by Eve Rice. Copyright © 1979 by Eve Rice. Reprinted by permission of Greenwillow Books, a division of William Morrow & Company, Inc.

"Pigsty" from PIGSTY by Mark Teague. Copyright © 1994 by Mark Teague. Reprinted by permission of Scholastic Inc. MONOPOLY is a registered trademark of Tonka Corporation for its real estate trading game and elements. Copyright © 1934, 1992 Parker Brothers, a division of Tonka Corporation. Used with permission.

"Martí and the Mango" from MARTÍ AND THE MANGO by Daniel Moreton. Copyright © 1993 by Daniel Moreton. Reprinted by permission of Daniel Moreton.

"A Fair Share" from FRACTION ACTION by Loreen Leedy. Copyright © 1994 by Loreen Leedy. Reprinted by permission of Holiday House, Inc. All rights reserved.

"The Paper Crane" from THE PAPER CRANE by Molly Bang. Copyright © 1985 by Molly Garrett Bang. Reprinted by permission of Greenwillow Books, a division of William Morrow & Company, Inc.

Unit 3 *Lights! Camera! Action!*: "The Enormous Carrot" from THE ENORMOUS CARROT by Vladimir Vagin. Copyright © 1998 by Vladimir Vagin. Reprinted by permission of Scholastic Inc.

"Celebration" by Alonzo Lopez, from WHISPERING WIND by Terry Allen. Text copyright © 1972 by the Institute of American Indian Arts. Reprinted by permission of Doubleday, a division of Bantam Doubleday Dell Publishing Group, Inc. Illustrations copyright © 1988 by Tomie dePaola. Reprinted by permission of G.P. Putnam's Sons, a division of Penguin Putnam Inc.

"The Swallow's Gift" from THE SWALLOW'S GIFT by Lindy Soon Curry, illustrated by Yumi Heo. Copyright © 1996 by Scholastic Inc. Reprinted by permission of Scholastic Inc.

"Music, Music For Everyone" from MUSIC, MUSIC FOR EVERYONE by Vera B. Williams. Copyright © 1984 by Vera B. Williams. Reprinted by permission of Greenwillow Books, a division of William Morrow & Company, Inc.

"Abuelita's Lap" from CONFETTI, A COLLECTION OF POEMS FOR CHILDREN. Text copyright © 1996 by Pat Mora. Illustrations copyright © 1996 by Enrique O. Sanchez. Reprinted by arrangement with Lee & Low Books Inc., 95 Madison Avenue, New York, NY 10016.

"The Bremen Town Musicians" from THE BREMEN TOWN MUSICIANS by Hans Wilhelm. Copyright © 1992 by Hans Wilhelm, Inc. Reprinted by permission of Scholastic Inc.

"Rubber Guitar" from THE SCIENCE BOOK OF SOUND. Text copyright © 1991 by Neil Ardley. Illustrations copyright © 1991 by Dorling Kindersley Limited, London. Reprinted by permission of Harcourt Brace & Company.

"Lights! Camera! Action!" from LIGHTS! CAMERA! ACTION! HOW A MOVIE IS MADE by Gail Gibbons. Copyright © 1985 by Gail Gibbons. Reprinted by permission of HarperCollins Publishers.

Photography and Illustration Credits